What Professionals Say about *The Learning Alliance*

"This book is the first of its kind to give serious recognition to the role and contributions of school psychologists working in a team effort to provide therapeutic care of our nation's school children.... The authors have provided a clear and consistent model for a 'learning-based psychotherapy that is applicable to a broad range of emotional, learning and behavioral based problems found so readily in urban schools.'"

—*Kirkland C. Vaughans, Ph.D.*
Editor, Journal of Infant, Child and Adolescent Psychotherapy

"...*The Learning Alliance* brings to the table everyone involved in the lives of children and adolescents in distress and helps psychiatrists to understand more fully life in the classroom. Teachers will appreciate the respect given to their daily important work. This book bridges the long-standing professional gap among those who work with students in distress. Students will read and then refer to *The Learning Alliance* regularly."

—*Nancy Belknap, Ed.D.*
Professor Emeritus, The George Washington University, Washington, DC

"This is a unique and practical book describing obvious, and not so obvious nuances of teacher-student-parent-therapist interactions. The authors take on several challenging tasks: to help the student succeed better in school; to help the teacher work more effectively with all students; to help the therapist work with the patient's complaints and difficulties with school work and school personnel; and to help the parent understand and help the child with school difficulties. It is the most superb synthesis of the consideration of mental health aspects of the classroom, the teacher, and the student that I have read in some time."

—*Irving H. Berkovitz, M.D.*
Editor, School Consultation/Intervention

"*The Learning Alliance* is a welcome orientation and guide for teachers, school administrators, and psychotherapists who work with children and adolescents. Good teamwork means communication among the players and everybody pulling together, not at cross purposes."

—*William Bernet, M.D.*
Professor, Department of Psychiatry, Vanderbilt University, Nashville, TN

"…By succinctly addressing and synthesizing the various dynamics or situations that cause a child to have difficulty in school, Dr. Meeks and Dr. Dupont offer clear concepts and practical steps for developing a "learning alliance" with students. Learning becomes a positive experience, thereby improving the child's self-esteem.… This superb book is a must-read guide for all psychotherapists who work with children and adolescents who 'hate school,' as well as school counselors, school administrators, school nurses, teachers, school-support staff, pediatricians, and parents."

—*Joan B. Goodman, LCSW-C*
Psychotherapist in Private Practice, Rockville, MD

"…There remained, of late, a void in the professional literature regarding the role and qualities of an effective psychotherapist in schools. Fortunately, *The Learning Alliance* fills that void with a must-read for educators and mental health professionals alike. Meeks and Dupont have produced a resourceful guide for anyone in the helping professions.… The authors have the central elements of school-based psychotherapy correct — build a therapeutic alliance that is focused on learning, fuel it with the process of identification, and sustain it over time with relationships based on caring, trust, and respect."

—*Howard S. Muscott, Ed.D., Professor*
Director of Undergraduate Special Education and the Graduate Programs in Educating Students with Emotional and Behavioral Disorders, River College, Nashua, NH

THE LEARNING ALLIANCE

Michael —
I hope you and your wife enjoy it. Thanks for keeping the author going.
John

Published by DMS Press
6000 Executive Blvd., Suite 605 Rockville, MD 20852

Copyright © 2003 by DMS Press. All rights reserved. No part of this book may be reproduced in any form or by any means, electronic, or mechanical, including information storage and retrieval systems, without permission in writing from the publisher. No liability is assumed with respect to the use of the information contained herein. Printed in the United Stated of America.

From a declaration of principles jointly adopted by a committee of the American Bar Association and a committee of publishers: This publication is designed to provide and authoritative information in regard to the subject matter covered. It is sold with the understanding that the publisher is not engaged in rendering legal, accounting, or other professional service. If legal advice or other expert assistance is required, the services of a competent professional person should be sought.

Book cover and interior design by Pneuma Books, LLC
For more information visit www.pneumadesign.com/books
Body set in ITC Giovanni 11|14pt. Titles set in Aldentor and Myriad

Publisher's Cataloging-in-Publication
(Provided by Quality Books, Inc.)

Meeks, John E.
    The learning alliance : a handbook for school-oriented psychotherapy / John E. Meeks and Philippe J. Dupont with the Foundation Schools staff. -- 1st ed.
    p. cm.
    Includes bibliographical references and index.
    ISBN 0-9719523-0-2

    1. School children--Mental health services. 2. Child psychotherapy. 3. Child psychotherapy--Parent participation. 4. School psychology. 5. Psychological consultation. I. Dupont, Philippe J. II. Title.

RJ504.M44 2002   618.92'8914
                            QBI02-701796

THE LEARNING ALLIANCE

A Handbook for School-Oriented Psychotherapy

John E. Meeks, MD
Philippe J. Dupont, EdD
with The Foundation Schools Staff

This book is dedicated to
Mary Jane Kennelly
for her management skills and
her tireless dedication and commitment to
The Foundation Schools

Acknowledgments

Many professional friends and colleagues have assisted us in the process of writing this book. Some supplied references, others read our various drafts over and over again, and others offered suggestions and recommendations. We have made it very clear, on our front cover as a matter of fact, that this book was written by the authors *with* The Foundation Schools. For twenty-seven years, many staff and students have passed through our school buildings, whether they were in Washington, D.C., Rockville, Maryland, Landover, Maryland, Leesburg, Virginia, or Alexandria, Virginia. They have been our teachers and our colleagues in the pursuit to find the best ways to teach and help children and adolescents with emotional disturbance.

We thank our life-long partners, Anita Meeks and Brad Davis, for supporting our efforts in creating this book for therapists, teachers, program assistants, related service personnel, parents, and families. Our administrative assistants, Cathy Maloney, Danita Moses, and Taricia Savage, have helped with the technologies of word processing, formatting, and e-mailing the drafts back and forth.

THE LEARNING ALLIANCE

For their counsel and constructive criticism, we especially thank: Andy Adler, Vice-President, The Foundation Schools; Stephen Banker; Nancy Belknap, Ed.D., Professor Emeritus, GWU; Ralph Bregman, Ed.D., Joan Goodman, LCSW; Sheila Kaler, Ed.D., Director of FSMC; Kelli, Kunert, Another Path; Addys Karunaratne, Ph.D., Director of FSPG; Denese Lombardi, M.A., Director of FSA; Joan Medway, LCSW, Ph.D.; Ruth Nolan, M.A., Director of FIS; and the program assistants at FSMC, specifically Joseph Green, Tony Miles, and Norris Jones.

Contents

Chapter 1
1
The Proper Function of Psychotherapy
in a School Setting

Chapter 2
17
Selling Children and Adolescents on the
Value of Education

Chapter 3
29
Identifying and Ameliorating Negative
Attitudes toward School

THE LEARNING ALLIANCE

Chapter 4
43
Helping Students Overcome
Negative Feelings toward Teachers

Chapter 5
57
Helping to Restore Hope
and Maintain Commitment

Chapter 6
67
The Role of the Family in
Academic and Vocational Success

Chapter 7
81
The Collaboration between
Therapists and Teachers

Chapter 8
93
Drug Use and Academic Work

Chapter 9
107
Creating and Maintaining
the Learning Community

Chapter 10
125
The Paraprofessional's
Role in School Psychotherapy

Contents

Chapter 11
139
The Office Therapist and
School Problems

Chapter 12
151
Tying It All Together

Bibliography
157

Resources
169

Index
175

About the Authors
193

Extra Credit Features

Extra Credit 1
11
Definition of Emotional Disturbance

Extra Credit 2
12
A Proposed New Definition of
Emotional or Behavior Disorder

Extra Credit 3
13
Chronology of Psychotherapists Who Influenced the
Education of Youth with Emotional Disturbance

Extra Credit 4
25
Occupational Wages in the United States, 2000

THE LEARNING ALLIANCE

Extra Credit 5
38
Reasons Students Report for Not Liking School

Extra Credit 6
39
What Students with
Disabilities Say They Like about School

Extra Credit 7
40
Behaviors Predictive of School Failure

Extra Credit 8
41
Recommendations to Improve
Students' Negative Feelings about School

Extra Credit 9
51
Strategies to Help Teachers Be More Effective with
Students with Emotional/Behavior Problems

Extra Credit 10
52
Boundary Defined

Extra Credit 11
53
Qualities of Children and
Adolescents Who Develop Clear Boundaries

Introduction

Extra Credit 12
54
Obstacles to Teaching Healthy Boundaries

Extra Credit 13
62
Hope Defined

Extra Credit 14
63
Nurturing Hope — Strategies for
Parents and Professionals to Enhance
Goal Development in Children and Adolescents

Extra Credit 15
64
Strategies for Parents and Professionals to
Enhance Children's and Adolescents'
Willpower Thinking

Extra Credit 16
65
Strategies for Parents and Professionals to
Enhance Children's and Adolescents' Waypower

Extra Credit 17
86
Ideas for Collaboration
between Therapists and Teachers

THE LEARNING ALLIANCE

Extra Credit 18
87
Therapist Standards and Expectations

Extra Credit 19
89
Teacher Standards and Expectations

Extra Credit 20
104
Stages of Adolescent Substance Abuse

Extra Credit 21
105
Another Path Program Tracks

Extra Credit 22
118
Two Forms of Bullying:
Aggressive and Passive

Extra Credit 23
119
Prevention, Intervention and Bullying

*You've got to
accent-tchuate the positive,
E-lim-my-nate the negative,
Latch on to the affirmative,
Don't mess with Mister in-between.*

*You've got to spread joy
Up to the maximum,
Bring gloom down to the minimum,
Have faith, or pandemonium
Li-ble to walk upon the scene.*

—Johnny Mercer & Harold Arlen, 1944

Suggested by Stephen Banker for use in *The Learning Alliance*. Popularized at staff developments by Nicholas Long

Introduction

The impetus to create this book came from a concern that many psychotherapists do not actively use their considerable skills and special influence to assist their child and adolescent patients in mastering the challenges of school. The lack of emphasis on academic issues in psychotherapy is particularly puzzling since such a high percentage of child and adolescent patients are referred to therapy because they are having difficulties in school. As a child psychiatrist and a special educator, we have pooled our experience to offer a general approach and some specific suggestions that may help therapists to approach this aspect of therapy more effectively.

It is our belief that effective learning occurs because a learning alliance is created and maintained. This alliance must include the student, his or her parents or guardians, teachers, paraprofessionals, other indicated specialists (such as speech/language pathologists, occupational therapists, art therapists, etc.), and the psychotherapist. The therapist is viewed as the facilitator and coordinator in the construction of the alliance. In addition, the therapist takes major responsibility for understanding and resolving those problems and attitudes that would prevent the student and the student's parents from committing to the educational process. It should be noted that this is not an alliance of equals. There are clear differences in the level of responsibility of its various members and differences in their authority. For example, the student is not prepared by experience or training to dictate curriculum, choice of teachers, or choice of schools. This is not to say that the student's opinions are ignored. The point is that the parent and professional educators are in the best position to choose the best options for the youngster. On the other hand, while the student is expected to eventually take responsibility for his or her educational effort, the load of responsibility is primarily on the teachers and therapists to guide the student through troubled times. The details of this complex collaboration constitute the body of this book.

This book originally was planned as an introduction for therapists working in The Foundation Schools, a special education program for children and adolescents with emotional disturbance in the Washington, D.C., metropolitan area. Several people who reviewed early versions suggested that it would also have value for therapists in other outpatient or residential settings in which schoolwork is an important element of the treatment program. Although the focus is on the role of the therapist, this book will be useful to all staff who are involved in creating the learning alliance, including teachers, program or teacher assistants, and administrators. Office practitioners may find it useful, at least in respect to the direct treatment of the young patient. Obviously, they may find themselves somewhat limited in their ability to implement some of the collaborative efforts with teachers and others that are described. On the other hand, some schools welcome therapist involvement and are quite responsive if approached with a respectful, collegial attitude. At the suggestion of several private practitioners, a chapter was added to address the situation of the solo practitioner. Finally, the book may be of interest to parents (not that they should attempt to provide psychotherapy to their children since parenting them is much more important) as a guide to generally productive ways to address their children's academic problems.

The approach to the student offered in the book can be briefly summarized as a sequential effort to assist youngsters in becoming effective learners. Although the stages are interdependent, and to some extent overlapping, the process can be thought of as having three steps with the initials AIM:

1. Aspiration — the measures taken to convince youngsters that education is important in their lives and worthy of their interest and labor
2. Inspiration — the process of helping the youngster to find his or her academic strengths leading to a personal expectation of academic success
3. Mobilization — the effort to help the student accept as well as develop appropriate work habits and strategies to make the learning institution helpful and supportive

We hope you will forgive us for saying, "That summarizes the AIM of this book."

The techniques suggested here are drawn from successful approaches used by therapists at The Foundation Schools over the years and from many students of learning — and the process of learning how to learn — who have written about their findings. Strayhorn (2002) has recently published two articles addressing self-control and its improvement in a variety of clinical situations. Self-control does not refer to suppression of feelings or expression. It refers to the capacity to delay immediate responses in order to gain a desired future goal. Strayhorn also provides an excellent review of the relevant literature. He, of course, recognizes the centrality of self-control for success in the school setting. Bandura (1997) coined the term *self-efficacy* to refer to the feeling of confidence that it is possible to achieve a goal. That confidence is the key to school success and to self-assurance and contentment in most aspects of life. Self-efficacy permits one to tolerate frustration and anxiety and to persist in a task. It is closely related to the factor we call *Inspiration*.

What does all this therapy stuff have to do with school?

1

The Proper Function
of Psychotherapy in a School Setting

There are many opinions about the proper objective of intensive psychotherapy — ranging from the grand and somewhat vague goal of restructuring the psychic makeup of an individual to the payment-driven specifics of convincing a patient to take medication or to at least stop talking about suicidal thoughts. This book proposes that, in the case of children and adolescents, an appropriate objective is to prepare youngsters to perform in school and the community at the level of their best ability. After all, Freud said that mental health could be evaluated through a person's ability to work and love. Later Anna Freud (1965) expanded on the transition from attachment to the mother to autoerotic play to ego-building play and finally to work. Certainly school is the workplace of young people, but it is also a major arena for play. The capacity to balance the two functions is essential to a well-rounded school experience.

The psychological requirements for academic success and social acceptance in the peer group are closely related to those aspects of personality that contribute to general adaptive competence. As a rule, these ego capacities also are associated with emotional well-being and general contentment. The good student who enjoys basic acceptance by his or her classmates is usually a happy person. On the other hand, most students who are unhappy and emotionally disturbed have difficulty with academics or with peer acceptance or both.

It is true that not all children with emotional problems perform below their potential. Some youngsters, especially those with neurotic or internalizing disorders can compartmentalize their pain and, at least on the surface, perform adequately in school. Even these students may benefit greatly from therapy that frees their creativity and curiosity. Indeed, early psychoanalytic writings on school problems — referred to as *learning inhibitions* — related the difficulties to conflicts around curiosity (Blanchard 1946). Conflicts of this kind still exist and one still sees youngsters who do not learn because they are obeying subtle parental messages that forbid growth and independence (Berger and Kennedy 1975).

There are still other young people who are totally caught up in intellectualization and some who are driven to obsessive efforts to achieve in order to please others. Problems can also appear if the academic expectations placed on the student are unrealistic for the child's age or ability. These more neurotic students need help in moving academics away from neurotic functions and toward a proper balance with life's other priorities, even if their good grades impress adults. School is a reasonable focus for therapeutic efforts whether the child is underachieving or unrealistically driving him or herself. Much of the school age child's life, meaningful interactions, and sense of accomplishment find focus in that setting. School is the laboratory of life and the setting where social, psychological, and mastery skills are tested in action and under observation.

Allen (1963) has observed: "In the (early) grades, the child is getting his first organized opportunity to find out what he can do as an individual, both with and against others. Here he learns how he can relate himself to others, meet the requirements of a school situation and do many things he would have no desire to do, except as they are required — develop his friendships in the group — restrict his own natural tendencies, talking, moving about, and so forth, to allow for group action. Here the child has the interesting and important problem of preserving his own individuality while yielding to the required aspects of the educational process."

Chess and Thomas (1986) make an even stronger statement. "The educational setting becomes a new center of struggle, adaptation and mastery, rivaling and even surpassing the significance of the home and playground for the youngster's development."

Each child brings special talents and particular issues to this daunting task. Some problems directly affect the learning process.

It is obvious that the capacity to attend to external stimuli with some degree of focus is basic to the learning process. Some psychiatric problems interfere directly with attention. The anxious or actively psychotic child is distracted from the learning process by overwhelming internal processes. Depression lowers energy, motivation, and cognition. Attention deficit disorder and other neurological disorders may impair attention or comprehension. It is important to recognize that all these deviations from average carry potential for special styles of comprehension that may not be open to the "normal" student. Langer, Piper and Friedus (1986) noted that dyslexic people were more creative in a problem-solving experiment. Other authors have noted that these students may have precocious and superior talents in nonverbal skills, such as art and architecture (Geschwind 1983; Porac and Coren 1981). However, when these conditions are unrecognized, they can wound the child in a typical school setting.

The basic attention disorders require active treatment that may include medication and special teaching approaches as well as psychotherapy (Denny and Rapport 1999; DuPaul and Rapport 1993; Abikoff and Gittelman 1985). The absence of appropriate early intervention can lead to other reactions that can be even more destructive to the learning process. In *The Explosive Child*, Ross Greene (2001) describes the basic difficulties that lead to frustration and failure if they are not ameliorated.

One might think of these basic attentional deficits as primary

...idemic failure. If they are not successfully remedied, ...d to secondary deficits. Secondary problems in learning are very common, even in youngsters without a predisposing primary psychiatric or cognitive disorder, or with only a minor one. Such problems can result from traumatic events, poor teaching, or inadequate supervision. A therapist working in a school program designed for children and adolescents with learning problems often must first deal with secondary, attitudinal blocks to education before the basic or original causes can be understood and ameliorated. This work is crucial but very difficult. The behaviors and beliefs that we identify as problems have been created by the student for self-protection and are not easily relinquished.

Essential Mental Attitudes

The ability to learn requires four basic mental attitudes:
1. *Aspiration.* The belief that learning is personally valuable.
2. *Inspiration.* Confidence that one has the skills necessary to learning.
3. *Mobilization.* The acceptance of necessary elements of the learning process.
4. The belief that the student's specific school situation can provide the necessary support for successful learning. (A final step in *Mobilization*).

Let's examine each of these elements.

The belief that learning is personally valuable permits the beginning of a learning alliance. Only the very young child will learn purely to please the loved adult. However, most students of any age are influenced by the example of adults that they admire. If parents, relatives, teachers, and other community adults value learning, the child tends to view education in a positive light as well. If they do not, the child may view school with disinterest or disdain. The desire to learn is further strengthened as the student understands the ways in which the educational process can aid personal achievement and growth in the present and the future. However, the stu-

The Proper Function of Psychotherapy in a School Setting

dent must also believe that he or she can succeed in the academic setting. True confidence can be based only on genuine achievement and perceived success. That point takes us to the third and fourth basic mental attitudes.

The recognition and then acceptance of the necessary elements of successful learning is a gradual process for all students. In some respects it parallels the development of the reality sense. The development of a sense of emotional competence begins during the toddler stage and requires both some confidence in one's capacity for mastery of novel situations and a comfort in accepting help from others when necessary. When this period of life does not unfold in a constructive manner (for example, if the caretaker is not supportive or conversely does not permit exploration) the child does not develop emotional competence. The youngster then lacks both a belief in his or her mastery skills and in the capacity of others to aid in skill development. These children are very anxious and to calm themselves often depend excessively on omnipotent fantasy. Since they are not omnipotent this leads them to avoid situations that force them to recognize any weakness because these topple their pretense and cause anxiety to return. These youngsters also reject dependency relationships of any kind. These two characteristics are major disadvantages in the academic setting, since effective learning requires admitting there is something that you do not know and that you need some guidance to learn.

On the other hand, when emotional competence is achieved there is hope that sustained effort can lead to success and that others, including adults, can be trusted to assist learning without risk of being demeaned. This developmental achievement allows the child to accept the fact that learning often requires hard work and often involves frustration and personal vulnerability. The pleasures of learning, especially as parents and other adults provide interesting and age appropriate stimulation, make the effort worthwhile. The work of learning becomes a higher level of play. The child is able to admit that there are many things she needs to learn that she does not yet know and can accept this fact without being overwhelmed

THE LEARNING ALLIANCE

by shame and anxiety. Such children have faith in themselves and in others and anticipate that the eventual outcome will be positive. Since their expectations are not grandiose they can enjoy minor triumphs and accept gradual progress. Much of the psychotherapy with troubled students involves a belated effort to rework these issues. As a group, they are impatient, easily frustrated by the slow pace of change, and uncomfortable and unskilled in using the help of others. In *Attachment Behavior and the Schoolchild*, Barrett and Trevitt (1991) provide an interesting guide to a treatment effort based primarily on attachment theory. It is especially useful in younger students but is an interesting theoretical approach. In the school they describe in England, psychotherapy is done by "educational therapists" and there is clear recognition that teachers often become the "specific attachment person."

Sometimes the source of learning problems can be obscured by these face-saving defenses, especially in bright youngsters.

> *Victor was referred for therapy because he was failing every subject in his sophomore year of high school. He had been a good student in elementary school but began to slide in middle school and now was hardly making any effort to complete his assignments.*
>
> *Victor told his therapist, "I just don't like to do the work. I really prefer to daydream."*
>
> *Victor's mother and stepfather were mystified. They felt Victor had a good relationship with them aside from their battles over his refusal to work in school. They reported that Victor just didn't care about school and seemed unfazed by his failure. Victor himself said, "That just doesn't affect my self-esteem. I know I'm okay."*
>
> *Although Victor's father died when Victor was two, he had quickly attached to the stepfather when mother remarried two years later. He called his stepfather "Dad" and had a warm bond to both parents.*
>
> *For a period of time, Victor maintained his disinterest*

The Proper Function of Psychotherapy in a School Setting

> *in school. He was placed in a psychotherapy group where other youngsters confronted him periodically, telling Victor that education was important and should not be dismissed. One day in group, to the surprise of everyone, Victor said, "You know, I can't concentrate in school. Not even when I try." The follow-up to the comment led eventually to a psychiatric evaluation and a diagnosis of Attention Deficit Disorder. Stimulant medication led to a rapid improvement in concentration. Continuation of psychotherapy allowed Victor to recognize and correct some of the poor work habits that he had embraced to avoid the feelings of helplessness and shame he had previously felt when he tried to address academic work. His fellow group members gleefully pointed out how proud Victor was of his new mastery of school. They had never believed that his self-esteem was unaffected by his failure.*

This case also illustrates the potential value of peers — in formal therapy groups or in a larger learning community — to the process of surfacing and reinforcing *Aspiration*.

Most youngsters who are referred to special education programs have an additional significant negative factor. As a rule, several efforts to solve their academic problems have already been tried and have failed. They are skeptical of any new effort. This makes their adjustment to the therapeutic program very difficult. Why should they risk another embarrassing failure?

The fourth essential element in learning is the development of a comfortable alliance with the student's specific school environment. This can be a major challenge for the student with special needs since the placement in an appropriate educational setting can itself be a narcissistic blow. He or she has officially been branded a failure. Often the student denies problems and displaces responsibility for the learning difficulties. It is common for the <u>first therapy</u> goal to consist of <u>convincing the student that the school is not the enemy</u>, or in fact the entire problem. "Everything would be fine, if I

THE LEARNING ALLIANCE

could just get out of this joint" is often the initial assessment offered by the student (Barga 1996; Brantlinger 1994). This attitude can be overcome only if the academic staff can demonstrate effectiveness in helping the student gain success and recognition of his or her academic, social, and vocational strengths. The staff must create an atmosphere that feels safe. This alone often wins over the student who is referred to special education because of emotional problems (Leone, et.al. 1990). The student must come to trust that he or she will not be at physical or emotional risk while endeavoring to learn. For one thing, this requires effective limiting of bullying and intimidation within the peer group. In a learning setting, it must be clear that there is a moral standard, which is not that "might makes right." If the "Code of the Street" (Anderson 1997) prevails, academic achievement will not be valued or sought. We discuss this matter at length in Chapter 9. Furthermore, the student must experience intermittent personal success. This requires effective remedial teaching, individually organized curriculum design, and creative teaching techniques. Again, see Greene (2001). Although the psychotherapist cannot impart these elements directly, therapists need to have an appreciation for these program enrichments. Therapists can help the angry and anxious student to recognize his or her potential value. This requires a dogged insistence on discovering the emotional, intellectual, and other strengths of the child. To whatever extent possible, the negative, disturbed, and failing aspects of the student are ignored. If they must be noted, they are discussed as temporary and correctable impediments to the eventual triumph of the student's strengths. The entire treatment team should steadfastly maintain a positive focus. The learning alliance is fueled by optimism and strengthened by every small evidence of progress. Treatment must be based on recognizing the strength and health in every student and enthusiastically supporting these aspects of the person.

This positive tone helps students to see their school placement as an opportunity, offered by a caring family and community in recognition of their worth and their potential. This can help them recover from the narcissistic blow of being identified as a "problem

The Proper Function of Psychotherapy in a School Setting

student." As mentioned previously, young people are strongly influenced by the attitudes of trusted adults — a position that the therapist usually enjoys. The therapist can help teachers reform the teaching-learning transaction by reducing that which is generally threatening to many students: criticism and pessimism. A coordinated treatment effort can lead most students to success even when they start far behind their age-mates.

Reasons for a Learning Focus in Psychotherapy

Three final reasons for a learning focus in psychotherapy:
1. This emphasizes a normative and healthy aspect of each youngster's functioning.
2. It is well accepted by the young person as a reasonable, objective, and respectable goal, less threatening than more clinical explanations of the purpose of therapy.
3. Doing poorly in school, for any reason, causes major problems in self-esteem and identity formation in the older student. As Cohen (1985) says, "The learning-disabled adolescent's conscious experience of self was commonly and consistently marked by feelings of incompetence, inadequacy, and the anxious anticipation of failure. However, the non-learning-disabled adolescents (who presented with various work or learning problems) often evidenced the same types of conscious concerns."

On the other hand, Silver and Hagin (1985) found in a long-term, follow-up study that, "the prognosis for academic achievement and occupational adjustment in children and adolescents who have the benefit of appropriate and sufficient educational intervention and receive optimal and necessary environmental support is favorable."

We now turn to a discussion of some of the day-to-day problems in assisting students to maximize their capacity for learning in school as well as the community. Of course, these approaches will be effective only if the therapist is able to gain a basic therapeutic alliance. As always this alliance is based on empathic understanding, careful attention to negative transference reactions, and the utilization of well-established therapeutic principles (Meeks and Bernet 2001).

As we address these methods, our simplified overall plan might be emphasized once again. In the busy and often hectic atmosphere of the school, we need all the help we can get for our effort to stay on track.

First, the student must be helped to find the *Aspiration* to academic success.

Next, the student must experience the feelings of confidence and *Inspiration* by discovering his or her academic strengths.

Finally, the student will need help in *Mobilization* through learning appropriate skills and attitudes to allow success.

Remember the three steps: AIM.

The Proper Function of Psychotherapy in a School Setting

Extra Credit 1

Definition of Emotional Disturbance

Many terms are used to describe emotional and behavioral disorders.

Currently, students with such disorders are categorized as having emotional disturbance, which is defined under the Individuals with Disabilities Education Act (IDEA), Public Law 101-476, as follows:

"The term means a condition exhibiting one or more of the following characteristics over a long period of time and to a marked degree that adversely affects educational performance:

(A) An inability to learn that cannot be explained by intellectual, sensory, or health factors;

(B) An inability to build or maintain satisfactory interpersonal relationships with peers and teachers;

(C) Inappropriate types of behavior or feelings under normal circumstances;

(D) A general pervasive mood of unhappiness or depression; or

(E) A tendency to develop physical symptoms or fears associated with personal or school problems."

(ii) The term includes schizophrenia. The term does not apply to children who are socially maladjusted, unless it is determined that they have an emotional disturbance."

(Code of Federal Regulations, Title 34, Section 300.7(c)(4))

Extra Credit 2

A Proposed New Definition of Emotional or Behavior Disorder

The term emotional or behavioral disorder means a disability characterized by behavioral or emotional responses in school programs so different from appropriate age, cultural, or ethnic norms that they adversely affect educational performance, including academic, social, vocational, or personal skills, and which:

- is more than a temporary, expected response to stressful events in the environment;
- is consistently exhibited in two different settings, at least one of which is school-related; and
- persists despite individualized interventions within the education program, unless, in the judgment of the team, the child's or youth's history indicates that such interventions would not be effective.

Emotional or behavior disorders can co-exist with other disabilities.

This category may include children or youth with schizophrenic disorders, affective disorders, anxiety disorders, or other sustained disturbances of conduct or adjustment when they adversely affect educational performance in accordance with section I.

(Forness and Knitzer 1992)

The Proper Function of Psychotherapy in a School Setting

Extra Credit 3

Chronology of Psychotherapists Who Influenced the Education of Youth with Emotional Disturbance

1925   August Aichorn publishes *Wayward Youth* pioneering that human attachment and relationships are key in the re-education process

1935   Loretta Bender founds school for psychotic children at Bellevue in New York City

1944   Bruno Bettelheim opens Orthogenic School at University of Chicago

1946   Fritz Redl and David Wineman open Pioneer House in Michigan

1953   Carl Fenichel opens the first private day school for students with emotional disturbance in Brooklyn

1960   Pearl Berkowitz and Esther Rothman co-write *The Disturbed Child*, using a psychoanalytical approach to education

1961   Nicholas Hobbs et al establish Project Re-ED in Tennessee

1962   Norris Haring and E. Lakin Phillips publish *Educating Emotionally Disturbed Children*

1965   Nicholas Long, William Morse, and Ruth Newman publish *Conflict in the Classroom*

1970   William Rhodes establishes *Conceptual Project in Emotional Disturbance*

1973   Hill Walker applies behavior principles to managing acting-out behavior in the classroom and promotes teaching social skills

continued next page...

THE LEARNING ALLIANCE

...continued from previous page
1990   Larry Brendtro, Martin Brokenleg and Steve Van Bockern introduce Circle of Courage, a holistic approach using a community-building model based on traditional Native American philosophy
1998   Nicholas Long, F. Fecser and Larry Brendtro rework Redl's *Life Space Interview* as *Life Space Crisis Intervention*

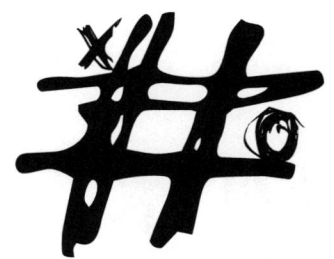

Who needs school anyway?

2

Selling the Value of Education
to Children and Adolescents

Many students doubt the relevance of school. "I don't care what those freaks did long ago." "Why do I have to learn all this fancy math? I can count and make change. What else will I ever need?" "Why should I do all this work when I'm not getting paid?" "School is so boring."

These comments usually contain some degree of sour grapes, coming from youngsters who have had major failures in their school efforts in the past. They are also to some extent simply the perfectly normal grousing about the fact that school is more work than play. As Allen (1963) put it long ago, "Since this period of growth (that is the early school years) finds the child in the process of determining and using his creative self and doing this under stimuli from without and within, the natural thing to expect is an ambivalent attitude toward teacher, curriculum, routine and other parts of the process. The rather natural response of the average child during this period is both to like and hate school. He accepts and fights it at the same time."

In spite of the reality of this observation, the therapist should

THE LEARNING ALLIANCE

take all negative statements about school seriously and sympathetically. One should not assume that every child has had the benefit of a thorough explanation of the function and importance of academics in human life. Some students may never have been taught why education should be a central element in their lives. Sometimes they have been told that learning is important but have been left to take it on faith. The learning alliance cannot occur until the student is convinced that the prize is worthy of the battle. Several actions can be taken to begin the process of enlightenment.

The first step in helping the student to understand the value of education is to provide some basic information, beginning at the most practical and materialist perspective. The student can be asked to guess the average annual salaries of people at different levels of formal education. How much per year does the average person who does not complete high school earn? How does that compare with the income of a high school graduate? Does the person who completes at least one year of college earn more? What about the earning power of the college graduate? What education or training do you need to land or advance in a particular job? Are there any benefits from education other than money? Business competition for skilled employees is causing what to happen in the United States? This is information that students deserve to have. Any misconceptions they may harbor should be corrected. If they have no idea of the facts, the information can be provided. We have included a chart we adapted from the U.S. Department of Labor Web site, www.dol.gov, to help students compare wages with required education or training.

Older students can also begin to consider other elements of the work experience as they relate to academic success. If the student considers school to be boring, ask him to consider the interest level in the repetitive, unchallenging job he will probably have to settle for without a degree. Often students recognize this in a more compelling way if they actually are employed for a period of time in a dull workplace. For the most part, the more mentally challenging, interesting jobs require a rigorous grounding on academics and

Selling the Value of Education to Children and Adolescents

workplace skills, including appropriate education/training in job specific skills. The danger is that the student will turn off altogether — to work *and* school

This is not to deny that there are some alternatives. Outstanding talent in the entertainment arts or athletics can lead to success without a solid formal educational background or more sophisticated types of work-based experiences. However, even in these cases young people are benefited by a solid fund of knowledge. Their education can help them negotiate the often-confusing world of public success and to manage their personal life wisely. It is rarely helpful to point out to the youngster that major success in these areas is very rare. Sometimes they can consider the fact that these careers are often relatively brief and that life after retirement will be improved by having a degree or certificate(s). At least this does not put the therapist in the position of just discouraging the youngster. Other students can comfortably entertain the idea of having a "back-up plan" in the event injury or other unpredictable factors foil their plans.

On a more realistic level, preparation in the skilled trades can offer a reasonable alternative to higher education, or the combination of skilled occupational training with post-secondary education is yet another alternative. The work of a plumber, construction worker, heavy machinery operator, or skilled mechanic can be very satisfying to young people whose intelligence tends more toward mechanical aptitude than book learning (Bregman 1976). However, even these students can understand that formal education may open greater opportunities in the trades. They can be asked for example, "What if you're extremely successful operating heavy machinery and turn out to be a natural leader? Do you want to be prepared to run your own company?" In addition the therapist should have information about the realities of achieving employment in these fields. Some require apprenticeship, which in most situations is very demanding and available only through a sponsor or after successfully completing trade school preparation. Apprenticeship opportunities for minority youth have lagged those available for whites (Sugar 1993).

THE LEARNING ALLIANCE

A student's belief that learning is boring should be actively challenged. Using one's intelligence and creativity to master new tasks and widen one's knowledge base is, in fact, one of the most engaging and entertaining of human activities. It is true that it is an active pleasure and requires expenditure of effort unlike the passive pleasures of TV and the destructive and illusory raptures of drug use, but it is demonstrably more pleasurable in the long run. We must communicate this fact with enthusiasm and conviction. This is not to say that we should lecture. Our clients are more impressed by matter-of-fact statements accompanied by actions that convey our beliefs. For example, noting a student's special interest and lending or giving her a book on the subject and discussing it with her is much more valuable than a righteous monologue.

Sometimes it is not clear why a student suddenly gains *Aspiration*.

> *Tanya was a seventeen-year-old senior who had been truant and severely drug involved for over two years. She had never had stable parenting. Parents had divorced when she was nine. Mother was alcoholic and promiscuous. Father was attentive to her whenever he did not have a current girlfriend only to drop her totally when he became enmeshed with still another woman. Tanya was tossed back and forth between the two parents and their ever-changing mates with little supervision or support.*
>
> *As a senior, Tanya was firmly but kindly confronted by a school counselor who referred her for evaluation. When Tanya presented herself to the therapist she said, "That was a wake-up call. I'm going to end up just like my parents if I go on like this."*
>
> *Almost immediately she quit drugs, dropped her drug-using friends, and struggled to catch up in school. With therapeutic support she persisted in this turnaround, graduated high school, and successfully completed a college education.*
>
> *Don't you wish it was always so easy? Sometimes maturity, reality, and a friendly push pull things together for a*

Selling the Value of Education to Children and Adolescents

> *youngster. Since one never knows which friendly push may help, we can only continue to offer them tirelessly and hope for the best.*

It is also important for the therapist to take a lively interest in the student's schoolwork. The proper role for the therapist concerning shared schoolwork is to be a cheerleader and a delighted consumer rather than a critic. The therapist is trying to help the student see the pleasure and value of schoolwork, not review its quality.

The therapist can also explore the student's dreams and plans for the future. At times these plans are very fanciful. The student intends to play basketball in the NBA although he has never played competitively at his grade level. Another student aspires to be a rock star even though she has never learned to play a musical instrument and is painfully frightened of performing before others. Such fragile dreams must be handled gently. The student is encouraged to talk fully and freely about her wishes, and especially about the rewards she anticipates deriving from accomplishing her ambition. It is worthwhile to ask about the history of the dream. How long has the youngster wanted to be in the WNBA? What events originated the thought? Gradually the therapist can inquire about immediate steps the student is taking to make the dreams a reality. The therapist can also inquire about the student's level of confidence that he can achieve their objective. "On a scale of 1 to 10, how likely are you to make it to the WNBA? Give me your best guess." "What changes in your habits would make it more likely for you to get there?" "Could anything happen that would cause you to change your goal?" Naturally, these inquiries should come up casually in a chat, not in the form of an inquisition. Sometimes it is possible to engage the student in further analysis about the desired rewards she has described. For example, if the student sees high income and fame as rewards, a conversation can ensue which points out that their current ambition is but one way to accomplish these rewards. There are many other paths they can take. Sometimes these discussions go to crucial clinical issues.

THE LEARNING ALLIANCE

> *Charmain, who was quite attractive, spoke constantly of her plan to become a mega-star. Her therapist assumed initially that the wish was related to narcissistic needs. Charmain was embarrassed by her ambition and wanted to dismiss discussion because, as she said, the reasons behind such a goal were obvious. Eventually she admitted that she believed that stardom was the only way that someone like her could get rich. When the therapist persisted in exploring her need to be wealthy, Charmain broke into tears and said, "I've got to do things for my mother. I owe her so much and all I give her is trouble."*

The therapist should remember that dreams do sometimes come true and not every seemingly grandiose scheme is cockeyed. To illustrate this, one of the authors was interviewing a new student in a special education program who stated that he intended to become a rapper. Further discussion revealed that the boy's uncle owned a record company and that the student had performed professionally several times and already had one album on the market! As the master said, "Assume nothing." It is also true that some vocational decisions appear at a very early age and persist: teaching, nursing, lawyering and doctoring. One of the authors met several people in medical school who had intended to become physicians for as long as they could remember.

Still, the usual history of early dreams is that they are gradually altered to approximate more closely the true talents and available opportunities as the child moves through adolescence. It is often the therapist's job to help students give up and mourn old and impossible dreams and to enthusiastically embrace new and achievable plans. Treating youngsters within the framework of school provides an excellent opportunity to identify strengths, aptitudes, and limitations so they can work toward a more rewarding identity.

Some students believe that the rewards of academic achievement are not available to them. They fear that racism, low socioeconomic background, or lack of influential sponsors will deny

Selling the Value of Education to Children and Adolescents

them opportunity for success no matter how much they are capable of. These concerns need to be discussed realistically and factually. There is a strong element of reality in these anxieties that will not be eradicated by facile denial of the major inequalities that exist in our society. However, exposure to successful role models with similar or even varied backgrounds at least opens the possibility that total pessimism is not justified and allows for hope. For the older student, personal experience is even more convincing. School vocational programs that place students in interesting jobs with intriguing opportunities for advancement can be powerful antidotes to nihilism. At times, the student gets the message in somewhat unexpected ways.

> *Monroe, a high school senior with modest academic skills, had done well in a work placement that involved skilled labor. However, he still struggled with shame over his mediocre grades. The students were taken to a stage production presenting the life of Dr. Ben Carson, the famous neurosurgeon. On the following day many students spoke of the inspiration they had found in the play. Finally, Monroe asked to speak. "What I learned from the play is that if you can use your hands skillfully, you will always have success," he said.*

A major focus for vocational education is building self-confidence in the individual student seeking to enter the adult world in a positive manner. "Work" in school in the form of projects and work-based activities at a business site are therapeutic. These experiences are most properly gained through a process whereby the student begins to seriously think about jobs and careers. The process of career development is formalized at school by learning about self, self in society, and the adult role envisioned (Bregman 1999).

These interventions alone will not usually convince the student that education is a crucial factor in a successful life or that school can be an engaging experience. The denial of the value of education

THE LEARNING ALLIANCE

almost always is defensive to some extent. The next chapter explores techniques designed to help students work through past negative school experiences, which have led to their abandonment of academic ambition.

It is unfair to the student for authorities to accept a negative attitude toward school without vigorous efforts to understand and alter that stance. If nothing else, the student is devoting huge amounts of time and energy to education and deserves some gratification from the effort. The student can be reminded of this fact when he or she complains that the therapist is now hassling them just like their parents and teachers. The therapist can point out that trying to understand and help does not really constitute meddling or nagging!

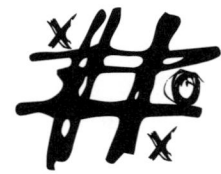

Selling the Value of Education to Children and Adolescents

Extra Credit 4

Occupational Wages in the United States, 2000

Occupation	$/hr*	Education Preferred
Actor	$24.71	degree preferred
Architect	$23.26	advanced degree
Artist	$14.06	degree preferred
Athlete	$25.24	degree preferred
Automobile Mechanic	$16.25	specialized training
Bank teller	$9.59	high school diploma
Brickmason	$20.91	specialized training
Bus driver	$12.98	training/license
Carpenter	$17.28	specialized training
Cashier	$7.66	on-the-job-training
Chief Executive Officer/ General Administrator	$23.73	degree
Child care worker	$8.74	high school diploma
Civil engineer	$27.35	degree
Computer operator	$14.83	specialized training
Computer programmer	$23.33	specialized training
Computer repairers	$17.17	specialized training
Computer systems analyst	$29.26	degree
Construction laborer	$12.35	on-the-job-training
Data entry keyers	$11.02	high school diploma
Dental hygienist	$26.07	degree
Dentist	$34.81	advanced degree
Driver, sales	$13.33	on-the-job-training
Electrician	$19.80	specialized training
Firefighter	$16.96	specialized training
Hairdresser/cosmetologist	$10.22	specialized training

continued next page...

THE LEARNING ALLIANCE

...continued from previous page

Occupation	$/hr*	Education Preferred
Heating, air conditioning and refrigeration mechanic	$15.71	specialized training
Janitor	$9.56	on-the-job-training
Laudering/dry cleaning machine operator	$7.69	on-the-job-training
Lawyer	$38.70	advanced degree
Legislator	$12.02	degree
Librarian	$23.28	degree
Maid/houseman	$7.80	on-the-job-training
U.S. Postal Service**	$20.62	passing qualifying exam
Musician	$28.69	degree
Nurse, licensed practical	$14.04	specialized training
Nurse, registered	$21.93	degree/specialized training
Nursing aide	$9.00	on-the-job-training
Painter	$13.98	on-the-job-training
Parking lot attendant	$7.75	on-the-job-training
Physician	$61.43	advanced degree
Pilot	$91.63	degree/specialized training
Police and detectives	$20.96	specialized training
Mail clerks, except postal service	$9.53	high school diploma
Psychologist	$27.20	advanced degree
Public relations manager	$37.20	degree
Receptionist	$10.14	on-the-job-training
Sales, business services	$19.62	specialized training
Sales worker, apparel	$10.02	on-the-job-training
Secretary	$14.31	high school
Social worker	$15.09	advanced degree
Speech therapist	$26.62	advanced degree
Stock clerk	$11.71	on-the-job-training
Teacher, college	$36.82	advanced degree
Teacher, elementary	$28.79	degree

Selling the Value of Education to Children and Adolescents

Occupation	$/hr*	Education Preferred
Teacher, secondary	$29.14	degree
Teacher, special education	$29.97	degree
Teacher aides	$10.17	high school
Truck driver	$12.95	special license
Waiter/waitress	$4.68	on-the-job-training
Welder	$14.52	specialized training

Source: National Compensation Survey: Occupational Wages in the U.S., 2000 U.S. Department of Labor Bureau of Labor Statistics September 2001

 * aggregated average national hourly earnings
** Statistic from U.S. Postal Service, 2002

I HATE school!

3

Identifying and Ameliorating
Negative Attitudes toward School

Disliking school is a learned reaction. Children typically enjoy their school experience in the wonderfully ambivalent way described in the earlier chapters. They like being with their friends. They enjoy learning new material and they like most of their teachers. Of course, they groan when summer ends and complain about getting up in the mornings. They also get bored during summer vacation and are quite ready to start school in the fall. They may drag their feet about doing homework and occasionally claim to be ill to miss a day. Nevertheless, overall, they would feel a huge void in their lives without the daily rhythms of school unless school is replaced by a lifestyle, such as farming or construction work, that provides a different daily rhythm.

For this reason, a true and abiding dislike of school should be viewed as a symptom. Often, expressions of hostility toward school may primarily be evidence of general unhappiness or of problems with peers. The school setting is a safe target. It is large, not immediately intimate, and, besides, hating school does not draw a lot of unwanted attention. *Everybody* dislikes school is the underlying supposition. On the other hand, there is the real possibility that the negative attitude toward school is educationally based and specifically focused on the academic institution. A careful workup is definitely in order to determine the source and evolution of school rejection.

Identification and Evaluation

The evaluation should begin with the student's first school experience whether it was nursery school, kindergarten, or first grade. Was there evidence of separation anxiety or other difficulty in leaving home for the new setting? If so, how was it handled and what transpired later? It is worthwhile to question parents/guardians about these events since youngsters may not remember early school experiences clearly. Moreover, it is important to assess the parents'/guardians' reaction to these important separation experiences as they represent major changes in family relationships. Early attitudes toward schoolwork and evidence of possible specific learning difficulties, such as a delay in learning to read, can show in these first years. The parents'/guardians' depth of knowledge about their youngster's school experiences and their response to any problems the child has encountered may hint at parental attitudes toward education and its importance. It is wise to avoid jumping to negative conclusions, however, as even committed parents may become discouraged over time and may retrospectively distort the past. A parent who is nihilistic and defeated in the present may forget previous good faith efforts.

The evaluation continues with a discussion of each school year. Interactions with teachers, positive or negative, subject preferences, and parallel events in the family or the child's history outside school should be noted. Special attention should be given to major family changes, such as geographic moves, illnesses, drug problems, divorce, separations, new caretakers, and deaths. It is particularly important to explore carefully any sudden changes in the youngster's attitude toward school. Early pleasure in learning can disappear simply because cognitive limitations become more troublesome as

Negative Attitudes toward School

school assignments become more demanding. Other students do well in the supportive setting of the self-contained classes of initial grades but have difficulty adjusting to the demands of relating to multiple teachers and the greater independence of later grades. However, most sudden changes in acceptance of school are related to interactions with teachers or other school staff in those situations where there has been no major external trauma.

Students' Perceptions of Teachers

The student's perceptions of his or her teachers over the years are very important data. Talking in detail about teachers the student has liked and those who were strongly disliked can be helpful in several respects. First, some students have encountered very toxic teachers — at least some particular teacher often can be identified as damaging in the interaction with this specific child. At times, such teachers eventually have been found incompetent in a public or formal way. More often the vulnerabilities of a particular student react badly with the teacher's particular tolerances and skills. In any case, the result for the student is traumatic.

Asking about favorite teachers can also yield valuable information. Why did the student like certain teachers? Was it that they were kind and supportive or because they helped the student achieve some academic success? It may be worthwhile to ask both questions. Who was your favorite teacher? Which teacher taught you the most? They are often, but not always, one and the same.

> *Sudden changes in the acceptance of school also can result from peer interactions.*
>
> *Robert disliked school intensely. He was truant occasionally, his homework had to be constantly supervised, and he was withdrawn and distant at home. In therapy, he finally admitted that he had liked school until the seventh grade when "something awful happened." It took several weeks of skirting the topic before he described being publicly humiliated by a bully while other students stood around laughing.*

THE LEARNING ALLIANCE

> *Salena, a popular sophomore, suddenly developed a sullen, depressed manner and neglected her studies. Her mother found her weeping but Salena denied she was upset. In a meeting with her mother and her therapist, she disclosed that one of her girlfriends had gotten angry with her and managed to turn most of her other friends against her. Once the conflict was addressed, Salena regained her previous good adjustment.*

It is also important to explore the student's feelings about specific subjects. Which study area is easiest? Which subject is most difficult? Which subject areas interest the student? Which subjects are most boring? Has the student ever had a teacher who could make the difficult or boring subject easier or more interesting? How did they do that? Discussing these questions may suggest the presence of specific learning disabilities or may suggest that negative attitudes toward a subject area are more related to personal conflict experiences and unrelated to cognitive problems.

Assessing Students' Confidence Regarding their Ability to Learn

While it is important to understand the chronology of the student's school experiences as they have impacted the youngster's attitude toward school, it is even more important to assess the murkier question of the student's level of confidence in his or her ability to learn. The true answer to this question is rarely apparent on the surface. Many students claim they can excel at school but that they just don't want to. Others say they are competent but that the work is so easy that it is boring or insulting so they refuse to lower themselves to do it. On the other hand some students claim to doubt their ability but actually they are understating their abilities to avoid the possibility of disappointing others or of being shamed. Often it is necessary to return to this area of exploration again and again. Facile claims of self-confidence can be gently challenged. The therapist might say, "That's really unusual: To never worry that things are too hard to learn. When I began long division I was

Negative Attitudes toward School

scared to death. I just couldn't understand it at first. I felt really dumb. It was very hard to even keep trying." Naturally, if the student can admit to any fear, the therapist quickly validates the experience. "Sure. School is like that. The moment you learn something they give you something you don't know. I think it's natural to have a lot of doubts and worries."

Some students claim they learn without doing homework or hard study. Again this has to be challenged actively. "I really don't understand. Most of the smart, really good students I know have at least an hour or two of homework every night. Are you sure you're getting all you should from your classes?" The student can be encouraged to bring homework into the therapy session as mentioned in the last chapter. Be forewarned: All of the therapist's skills may be tested in convincing the youngster to agree to this idea. If the student can be nagged, cajoled, or otherwise influenced to allow the therapist to participate in this part of his or her life, the experience can be very useful. Watching a child do homework provides an excellent opportunity to observe defenses of denial, avoidance, and misdirection in action. The anxieties and fears behind these evasions may also be revealed. The student is usually worried that he will appear dumb and needy — spoiling a cool image he worked very hard to project. Gradually and gently, the therapist can confront the student with a more realistic appraisal of his or her feelings about personal academic strengths and weaknesses. This undertaking requires friendly persistence in the face of the student's wishes to dismiss the subject as unimportant while offering many more interesting alternative topics. At some point, one can initiate the long, difficult effort to help the student face her fears honestly and to overcome her academic difficulties with courage, hope and hard work. One should expect the student to resist this work energetically. It is frightening to give up the comfort of omnipotent fantasy and accept the fearful uncertainty of maturation and learning. The therapist should be prepared for many setbacks, armed with a supply of confidence, hope, and support that the student will need to draw on during difficult periods.

THE LEARNING ALLIANCE

In some cases, therapeutic persistence may be as valuable as therapeutic skill.

> *Carly, age fifteen, and her fourteen-year-old sister began to spin out of control when they began smoking marijuana regularly during the summer before Carly's sophomore year. In that year, Carly's school performance collapsed totally. She and her sister regularly slipped out of the house at night. They both failed all their classes and Carly dropped out of school. Residential placement and multiple hospitalizations did not curb Carly's self-destructiveness. An outpatient therapist stayed in contact and met with Carly whenever possible.*
>
> *A short time later, Carly and her sister broke into a neighbor's home and took the keys to two automobiles. They took them joyriding and totaled* both!
>
> *The court sent her to a drug treatment center for forty-seven days, then put her on house arrest and continued mandated treatment in a day treatment hospital. During this close containment, she stopped drug use but freely admitted to her therapist that she missed "drinking and drugging."*
>
> *With this apparent improvement, the court relaxed control and sent her to a therapeutically oriented school designed to help drug-involved youngsters. She quickly got into conflict and was expelled from the school. The court sent her back to juvenile detention. Her outpatient therapist visited her there for a session. Carly was amazed and touched that her therapist had not given up on her. That session marked a turning point in her treatment. Carly now accepted medication and cooperated in therapy sessions. She completed high school and entered a local college. At follow-up, she admitted to some sporadic drinking, but was performing adequately — though not to her full potential — at college while holding a full-time job.*

Negative Attitudes toward School

Sometimes the dislike of school is an expression of family conflict or rebellion and has little to do with difficulties in the educational setting. For example, if a parent is performance-oriented and focused on external badges of success, such as grades or election to school offices, the student may fight the pressure. In other situations, school success can fall victim to neurotic inhibitions.

> *Arthur was an excellent student through the early grades. His hard-working father held high standards for Arthur and, although he worked two jobs, he supervised the boy closely. He was determined that his son would use education to escape the ghetto.*
>
> *A few weeks into high school, Arthur suddenly changed. He neglected his assignments, argued with teachers, and declared that school was a "bunch of BS." Everyone was shocked and therefore tried to remonstrate with Arthur.*
>
> *After a few days of this, Arthur lost patience and screamed at his favorite teacher. "You are all just like my father. You expect way too much!"*
>
> *His therapist followed up on the comment for several sessions with no real benefit. Finally, the therapist got irritated. "Arthur, your father loves you and cares about you. Why are you suddenly so angry?"*
>
> *Arthur broke into tears. "I'm going crazy!" he said. "Every night I have the same nightmare. Some thugs in our neighborhood break into our house. They're going to kill my Dad and my sister and I can't stop them. I'm afraid to go to sleep. I'm exhausted."*
>
> *Gradually Arthur was able to explore his ambivalent attitudes toward his father. As he did so, his capacity to learn returned.*

Situations such as Arthur's are fairly common and the therapist must be alert to hidden and sometimes complex psychodynamics. However, the most common story to emerge from the evaluation of a student's hostility to school is far more difficult to resolve. Most students who dislike school have encountered academic failure in the past. Whether the failure resulted from an unrecognized and untreated cognitive defect, unskilled teaching, or external disruptions of the educational experience, the negative result begins a self-perpetuating cycle of unhappy events. The student's attitude becomes less compliant, teachers react to the student's provocation, and the problem escalates. By the time several years have passed, the expectations match the eventual disruptive outcome.

Learning Disabilities as Barriers to Academic Success

Cohen (1985) has said of the child with a learning disability, "This experience of feeling emotionally injured resulting from repeated moments of helplessness, inadequacy and pain does not seem to be an immediate response in childhood. I have not observed it in most learning disabled children under the ages of seven or eight." However, as time goes by, a typical clinical picture emerges, as described by Garber (1992): "Learning disabled adolescents, even those who have experienced years of assistance, do not understand what their specific cognitive disability was and is or how it affects their social interaction and learning. It is difficult to differentiate the actual effect of the disability from the meaning that they have given to it. As a result, learning disabled adolescents believe that there is something seriously damaged in their heads." Cohen (1985) says of the group of adolescents with learning disabilities he studied, "A surprisingly high number of the students studied attempted to compensate by utilizing avoidance strategies (including plagiarism)." Is it really surprising, considering the feelings described above? [2B]Nonetheless, even if expectable, this proclivity toward avoidance perpetuates the failure to learn. It is the therapist's task to keep the problem in focus without exceeding the student's ever-changing tolerance for anxiety. Garber (1992) discusses the maneuvering and testing these students display. "The various maneuvers are means of dealing with an environment that may be ambiguous or confusing, The more intelligent the adolescent, the more complex the testing

Negative Attitudes toward School

maneuver. These testing maneuvers, which try the patience of parents, teachers, and therapists, often obscure the learning disabled adolescent's strengths and capabilities." The therapist must help everyone — especially the student — to see through this tangled web to find the scholar within.

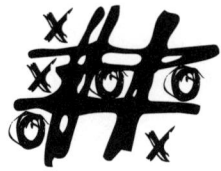

THE LEARNING ALLIANCE

Extra Credit 5

Reasons Students Report for Not Liking School
- Not having enough opportunities for social contact
- Being treated like a baby
- "Disconnectedness" from significant others
- Feeling like they don't belong
- I'm not a good student (feeling incompetent)
- It is boring
- Lots of "baby" work
- It's not important
- Teacher only teaches one way (lecture)
- Too many rules

(Habel, Bloom, Ray, and Bacon 1999)

Extra Credit 6

What Students with Disabilities Say They Like about School

1. 47% reported they like non-core curriculum classes like vocational, physical education, etc.
2. 41% reported they liked their academic classes like Math, English, Social Studies, etc.
3. 12% reported they liked electives such as art, language, etc.
4. 40% preferred special education classes because more help was available, class size was smaller and classes were easier
5. 80% reported they liked receiving individual help from their teachers
6. 12% reported they liked receiving help from their peers
7. 14% reported they liked receiving help from teacher aides
8. 5% reported they liked receiving help from noninstructional personnel, educational specialists or "myself"

(Lovitt, Plavins, and Cushing 1999)

Extra Credit 7

Behaviors Predictive of School Failure
- Overly dependent on teacher for direction
- Teases and interferes with others
- Concentration and attention difficulties
- Comes to class unprepared
- Becomes upset under pressure
- Works impulsively
- Lacks self-confidence
- Highly opinionated
- Unreceptive to others' opinions
- Nervous, anxious, and withdrawing

(Kauffman 2001)

Behaviors Predictive of School Success
- Establishes rapport with the teacher
- Responsive in class
- Engages in conversation with teacher before and after class
- Asks relevant questions
- Participates in class discussions
- Completes more than minimum work required
- Follows directions
- Exhibits originality and reasoning skills
- Arrives to class prepared
- Prepares homework in an interesting way

(Kauffman 2001)

Negative Attitudes toward School

Extra Credit 8

Recommendations to Improve Students' Negative Feelings about School

- Assist students to be more independent
- Make students aware of how special education is meant to help them
- Present students with a variety of post-school options
- Teach social skills
- Focus on student strengths
- Work on basic skills of reading, writing, and math

(Lovitt, Plavins, and Cushing 1999)

I hate that bitch.

Helping Students
Overcome Negative Feelings toward Teachers

Many students with academic problems have some degree of hostility toward teachers. After all, their school experiences have often been frustrating and embarrassing. Since teachers are required to set tasks and to evaluate their completion, they are often a source of pain to the struggling youngster. In addition, the rejection of learning and the disruption of the classroom, which are often defensive measures of the child or adolescent with academic difficulties, are behaviors that strike at core values of the educator. The therapist must often tread a thin line, accepting the student's expression of negative feelings while attempting to amend them, at the same time trying to help teachers recognize the true source of the youngster's resistance. Even older adolescents have trouble doing their best work for teachers they dislike. Accepting assignments, allowing corrections, and feeling enthusiasm for the subject matter is difficult if one sees the teacher as an enemy or a threat.

It can be difficult for the therapist to be an effective aide to the student in working out conflicts with teachers. It is a bit awkward to be put in the middle when one has no way to gain totally objective information. It is also an emotional topic even when generalized. Hot debates swirl around the question of whether our children are being properly taught and the conclusions can range from harsh critiques such as *Dumbing Down Our Kids* (Sykes 1995) to impassioned defense such as *The Manufactured Crisis* (Berliner and Biddle 1995).

Most studies of discipline management in the classroom have focused on comparing teachers' attitudes and behavior on a continuum from "custodial" to "humanistic." Most studies have found that the humanistic approach is not only better accepted by the students but also leads to better academic performance (Allen 1986; Lunenberg and Schmidt 1989). However, individual students may react differently based on their situations and experiences. For example, Bodine, et al. (2000) found that a group of adjudicated youth who were placed in residential detention did not look favorably on rewards – usually part of a humanitarian approach- and did not react badly to close supervision – often viewed as more custodial. Again the therapist is well advised to stay objective and to individualize each situation without making any early judgments.

The therapist needs to accept any negative feelings about teachers that the student presents without agreeing with them. If pressed for an opinion the therapist should reply honestly but in support of the teacher's function. For example, one might say, "It sounds like you're having a lot of trouble with Mr. Jones. I guess he can be strict but many students tell me they learn a lot in his class. Let's try to figure out a way to make things better." Sometimes the student is too angry to discuss the situation when it first comes up. In that moment the student may just be adamant about getting out of the teacher's class. The therapist needs to listen but shouldn't get directly involved in that issue. It can be useful to point out that a class change may disrupt the student's schedule in other negative ways, perhaps requiring giving up a favorite teacher or a required subject. However, the therapist can help the student gain an interview with the staff member in charge of scheduling. The very nature of the process allows for some delay, which allows time for calming down.

Helping Students Overcome Negative Feelings

As the student's anger recedes, he or she may be able to weigh the advantages or disadvantages of insisting on a class change. The therapist can also point out that many students get off to a bad start with a particular teacher and later find the teacher very helpful if they are willing to persist. The main purpose of these interventions is to get beyond emotional invective so that the therapist can explore the reasons behind the hostility.

For example, if the therapist knows from earlier investigation that the student finds mathematics very difficult it would not be surprising if the youngster had difficulty getting along with the math teacher. Anger is an excellent disguise for embarrassment, fear of failure, or anxiety related to a topic. This possibility is always important to explore. It may be more difficult to identify in elementary grade students since one or two teachers often teach all subjects. Of course, in that situation discovering the problem subject is even more crucial since dislike of one's only teacher is devastating to the entire learning process. In early grades, problems in thinking styles or cognition are often the reason for upsets and anger (Greene 2001).

In other cases, there can be genuine personality conflict between the student and the teacher. Some students have pretty much declared war on all teachers. Since they expect to be defeated on the academic battlefield, they launch a preemptory strike, vilifying the teacher before they can be criticized. This tendency should have been recognized in the historical evaluation of the student's previous school experience described in the previous chapter. Armed with the background knowledge the therapist can gently recall the student's long history of painful school experiences that have made it difficult to give any teacher a chance to be helpful. The student can be reminded of the advantages of gaining an education and the need to work cooperatively with teachers in order to reach that goal. The student can be encouraged to focus on the shared educational goal and reminded that the teacher's actions, such as giving instructions, assigning work, or asking for appropriate classroom behavior, are aimed at aiding learning, not at demeaning or humiliating the

THE LEARNING ALLIANCE

student. Mediation with the teacher may help the student to see the teacher's positive intent and allow the student and teacher to explore together effective strategies for their classroom interaction.

Occasionally, teachers may need help in understanding the student's unjustified anger and rebellion. The therapist can accept the teacher's frustration as understandable. Studies have demonstrated that even well-meaning teachers tend to withdraw and feel less positive toward behaviorally difficult students (Abidin and Kmetz 1997). The teacher's professional training and experience will help her to eventually understand how the student's school history and particular problems can lead to maladapted classroom attitudes, but she may benefit greatly from the enlightenment offered by the therapist's knowledge of the situation.

Sometimes, however, the situation is more complicated. When the friction is more personal, apparently unrelated to subject matter, and not generalized, the problem can be more difficult to diagnose and resolve. Sometimes the teacher is a part of the impasse. Fortunately, teachers are human. Their emotions allow them the enthusiasm, personal investment, and demonstration of feelings that help them connect to their students. The same humanity opens the possibility of countertransference, those idiosyncratic emotional responses that derive from our previous experiences rather than the reality of the current interaction. For example, a male teacher who grew up with a dominating older sister might tend to overreact to aggressive and self-assertive female students. Their healthy challenges and potentially positive arguments and discussions might be experienced as disruptive attacks on his authority.

The therapist needs to be open-minded and even handed in sorting out conflicts between students and teachers. If the teacher seems to be having a personal problem with the student, the therapist will be faced with the delicate task of helping the teacher become aware of somewhat hidden feelings. This is easier to do if the entire staff has permission to voice their honest feelings — even when they are unprofessional. Such an atmosphere does not condone unprofessional behavior. Each staff member is given permission to feel the

Helping Students Overcome Negative Feelings

whole range of human emotions but expected to process the feelings sufficiently to maintain his or her proper role with the students. Once feelings are out in the open it is not necessary in most cases to subject the teacher to further analysis or personal revelations. Detaching the reaction from the student allows the teacher's professionalism to take control once again.

The therapist may then have to be sensitive to the possibility that the student may have been drawn into playing the other half of the irrational and unhealthy interaction. Even when the teacher returns to appropriate classroom behavior the student may persist in efforts to recreate the negative interaction. The therapist can be helpful by describing the situation in words the student can understand. For example, "I know you were feeling that Mr. Jones was always putting you down and not listening to your views. Now I understand he is 'bragging on you' and has made you head of the debating team. But still you're in his face about every little thing. Are you still angry or is this just a habit now?" Of course, this isn't delivered as a lecture but is imparted bit by bit when there are appropriate openings.

Still, most student-teacher conflicts are mainly related to problems the child or adolescent brings to the classroom setting. A common situation involves the emotionally immature student. These students often have a honeymoon of positive feelings toward new teachers but gradually become more negative. Their initial enthusiasm is based on the hope that the teacher will meet their tremendous dependency needs and provide unconditional love. Since teachers typically are warm and affectionate, especially in response to the friendly approach these students initially present, the fantasy is understandable. Like all fantasies it is doomed to be ground away by reality. The gradual realization that the teacher gives attention and support but also expects work from the student spoils nirvana. The further realization that one has to share the teacher's affection and attention with all the other students is also distressing. To compound the disillusionment the teacher may even have to point out the student's mistakes! Disappointment breeds anger and the student complains that the teacher "doesn't like me." The therapist has an excellent opportunity in this interaction, to deal with sibling rivalry, painful dependency yearnings, the requirement to be personally productive, and the sometimes unwelcome necessity to share good things with others. The teacher may need help in understanding the student's deteriorating relationship and in realizing that it is not the result of wrongdoing. The only crime was doing the job properly. In so doing the teacher has made manifest a failure in maturation, which needs to be actively and sympathetically addressed.

Boundary Issues
In the process of investigating student-teacher conflicts, the therapist should also be alert to possible boundary problems. Students or even teachers may be drawn into attachments that are not compatible with a proper learning alliance. Whether these are romantic, parental, mutually protective, or narrow identifications, they are not conducive to accomplishing the educational goal. As a rule these attachments are readily apparent to the other students who resent the special status and favoritism given the chosen student. Other staff members also sense the intensity in the teacher's bond with the student. Frequently they tease the teacher and may also resent the student. The therapist has a more serious role. It is the therapist's responsibility to address the problem directly. A careful investigation is essential. If there is any evidence of grossly unprofessional behavior on the part of the teacher, that suspicion must be communicated to the school administration before any further damage occurs to the student. If it becomes clearer that the teacher's behavior is unethical, firm action must be taken to stop the inappropriate behavior. If the issue is more subtle and less damaging to the student, such as giving gifts, excessively protecting the student, praising the student extravagantly, or otherwise stepping outside the proper educational role, it is more likely a matter for tactful but honest discussion. We have all been guilty of being too narcissistically invested in a client's achievements, too proud of a patient's progress, or

Helping Students Overcome Negative Feelings

too angry at a therapeutic setback. If we are to remain objective and professional we need the candid feedback that others can offer.

Finally, the teacher sometimes is a victim of his or her success. Paradoxically, the very skill the teacher brings to the instructional process can threaten some students. These students have deep fears of being wounded by people that they trust or depend upon. Such fears are often well grounded in their experiences with people whom they counted on. A friendly, skilled teacher may become a dangerous temptation on an emotional level. Once again the youngster is drawn toward a dependent bond. Even though this is an appropriate, self-chosen dependency, the *once burned* child may not be able to make this distinction. The result can be a deliberate attempt to force the teacher to behave in a hostile or rejecting way so that the student can maintain emotional isolation and safety. If the student can succeed in pushing the teacher away, she again has proven that no one can be trusted so she does not have to risk being hurt. It is again the destructive power of the long shadow of early problems in the attachment, separation, and individuation phases of early childhood — especially the period that Mahler et al. (1975) named rapprochement.

The therapist has a major responsibility to recognize this situation and then to make every effort to correct it. The student has the opportunity to understand and master a defensive trait that is at the core of previous failures and that will continue to be destructive if not corrected. The teacher has the chance to overcome a common classroom interaction that has driven many talented teachers out of the field.

The therapist should intervene with the teacher as soon as possible. The teacher needs reassurance she is doing a good job with the child and she needs help to avoid being pulled into the negative interaction that the student is driven to create. If the teacher can avoid reverting to sarcasm, anger, or avoidance in dealing with the student, the therapeutic work with the student is much easier.

The therapist can focus on the student's ambivalence toward the teacher, perhaps recalling positive comments from the past. Unfair or inaccurate accusations should be questioned. Many times the student will claim that the teacher is only pretending to be nice while actually harboring secret hostility. <u>The therapist should ask for evidence and examples, not in a challenging way, but only in a patient effort to understand.</u> The therapist might even say, "I'm especially curious about this because Mrs. Smith seems so straightforward to me."

The therapist needs to be alert to evidence that the student is afraid the teacher has too much power or influence over her. The student may also complain that the teacher wants to take too much credit for any successes the student may enjoy. These issues provide the opportunity for the student to recognize the value of choosing to be temporarily dependent in order to achieve a goal that eventually increases the capacity to be independent. The student may also be able to identify the fear of trusting anyone and do useful work around the painful events that created this anxiety.

Helping Students Overcome Negative Fe

Extra Credit 9

Strategies to Help Teachers Be More Effective with Students with Emotional/Behavior Problems

- Establish clear classroom rules the first week of school (no more than five!)
- Distribute copies of classroom rules to students and parents so expectations are clear
- Design classroom environment that is attractive and pleasant
- Show genuine interest for each individual student in your classroom
- Create a caring and psychologically safe classroom environment
- Model appropriate behaviors you want your students to own
- Teach appropriate social skills while you are teaching academic content
- Maintain healthy boundaries with students
- Respect diversity in your actions and in your words
- Call attention to your students' acts of kindness
- Provide frequent praise and positive feedback
- Use a variety of teaching methodologies
- Be honest and upfront with your students
- Telephone parents/guardians with positive news at least once a month

THE LEARNING ALLIANCE

Extra Credit 10

Boundary Defined

A boundary is a "property line" that defines a person; it defines where one person "ends" and someone else "begins."

If we know a person's boundaries, we know what we can expect this person to take control of him/herself. We can require responsibility in regard to feelings, behaviors, and attitudes.

A child or adolescent needs to know where s/he "begins" and "ends," what s/he needs to take responsibility for, and what s/he does not need to take responsibility for.

Children are not born with boundaries. Boundaries are learned. Children and adolescents internalize boundaries from their relationships and discipline.

(adapted from Bluestein 1993; Whitfield 1993)

Helping Students Overcome Negative Feelings

Extra Credit 11

Qualities of Children and Adolescents Who Develop Clear Boundaries

- A well-defined sense of who they are and what they are responsible for
- The ability to choose and make good decisions
- The understanding that if they choose well, things will go well and if they choose poorly, things will go poorly
- Products of well-defined boundaries: self-control, responsibility, and freedom

(adapted from Bluestein 1993; Whitfield 1993)

Extra Credit 12
Obstacles to Teaching Healthy Boundaries
- Dependence on the child/adolescent
- Over-identifying with the child/adolescent
- Thinking that caring and separateness are enemies
- Believing there isn't a problem
- Believing the child/adolescent can't make it without you

(adapted from Bluestein 1993; Whitfield 1993)

Helping to Restore Hope
and Maintain Commitment

The school schedule with its annual summer break, grade promotion schedule and changes in school placement lends itself to new beginnings. Like New Year's Eve, there are annual opportunities to begin anew with resolutions for self-betterment. In September all things seem possible, even effortless. Soon this confidence fades and the realities that have slowed or blocked progress in the past have to be faced yet again. This is when the therapist is again challenged to help the student to learn the value and the techniques of perseverance.

Setting Realistic Goals and Clear Expectations
Many students with academic problems recognize that they need an education. They are fairly clear on their *Aspiration*. Unfortunately, they often rely on a vague idea that things will magically change and they will catch up with their successful peers. They are not genuinely *Inspired* since they have no solid basis for confidence in their efficacy. So when their fantasy is threatened they may simply ignore the issue or decide to drop out of school and

THE LEARNING ALLIANCE

turn their attentions elsewhere — rarely to a constructive course. It is the therapist's duty to lead the school staff in an all out effort to prevent this unhappy outcome.

First of all, it is important to be sure the student is setting realistic goals. In collaboration with the youngster's teachers one needs to be sure that the student's assigned schoolwork is at an appropriate skill level and that appropriate remedial techniques are provided. Obviously, if the student is expected to perform tasks that are beyond her abilities, no amount of therapy can change the resulting failure and discouragement (Greene 2001).

The next area to explore is the student's subjective experience. How realistic are the student's performance expectations? How accurate is the student's assessment of his or her work? Many students with academic problems are impatient and easily discouraged. Often they have unrealistic dreams that their learning problems will vanish because they have worked diligently for a week or ten days. Sometimes they believe that a short burst of effort will suddenly make them brilliant scholars. When victory does not come easily they may blame themselves although they may vocalize resentment toward assignments or teachers. This is a good time for the therapist to clarify how success is actually achieved: not through brief intense labors but through methodical, sustained effort. The therapist can also give the youngster permission to have *bad days* and to accept the normal ebb and flow of energy and motivation. Examples from sports or show business can help the student to see that no one triumphs magically. It may also be helpful to remind the student that even these stars have setbacks. The best hitters strike out and the best football players fumble. They do not quit because they made a mistake. Paradoxically, it can sometimes be helpful to join in cheerfully when the student is complaining about how hard he or she is working. The therapist might say, "Man, I know what you mean. I was ready to drop out of school more than once. Of course, now I'm glad I didn't. But at the time I didn't think I could make it another day."

Helping to Restore Hope and Maintain Commitment

Reviewing Progress with the Student

During periods of discouragement it is often helpful to the student for the therapist to review the real progress the student has achieved. "I understand that you're in a hurry to do even better but remember last year you couldn't stand to stay in class for the whole period and you never did your homework. Now you're on your case because you made one D. I'm confident that you'll continue to improve but there will be bumps along the way." It is also important to rework the student's clarity of purpose and reemphasize the internal motivation. "Naturally the rest of the staff and I are very proud of the progress you've made but I want to check with you. How about you? Are you proud of yourself? Do you feel good about your work? That's even more important. That's what will keep you going on a tough day."

The therapist can also encourage the student to bring schoolwork into the therapy session. This provides the opportunity to give direct praise and encouragement and to show enthusiasm for the content of the student's studies. It can be helpful at times to let the student tutor while the therapist takes the student role and learns or relearns subject matter. The therapist should aim to make learning a pleasurable, shared activity. This direct awareness of the student's work also allows the therapist to publicly praise the student's accomplishments, ideally in conjunction with the student's teachers. This approbation must be accurate and realistic, perhaps particularly lavished on the student's stubborn perseverance in the face of difficulties. Students with emotional learning problems have major holes in their academic self-esteem. One can hardly be too generous in recognizing their genuine progress. Teachers can also make a concerted effort to praise these students. But at the same time it is important to remain aware of the similar needs of the student's classmates. Praise needs to be spread around to avoid excessive envy or resentment of "teacher's pet."

Finally, it is important to mobilize all available external support. Parents and guardians should be kept aware of the student's achievements and victories. They should be helped to adopt a pos-

THE LEARNING ALLIANCE

itive approach, but encouraged to provide a home structure that formalizes time for homework and expects the student to utilize it. When the student is going through periods of discouragement and lowered motivation the parents should be informed and urged to offer additional support. Since the parents of youngsters with school problems have often been harassed and blamed by frustrated school officials in the past, it is important to make every effort to maintain a positive, optimistic, and collaborative tone in interactions with them. Rather than calling them with the blunt message, "Johnny is not doing any of his work. He will flunk everything if he goes on like this," it may be more productive to take a more positive slant. "I'm calling because I need your help. We're all trying to help Johnny through a rough time right now. As you know he was really trying and making some progress. Lately he's getting discouraged and he's tempted to just give up.

We're doing several things to see if we can get him over this rough spot and I had a couple of ideas for things you could do to help. Mind if we toss them around for a bit?" In some cases, outreach services with home visits may be indicated, especially if the slump includes increased truancy. At times older siblings, other relatives, ministers, coaches, or other community members can be helpful in strengthening the student's resolve and enthusiasm. Perhaps it is not so much what any of these people, including the therapist, say. Perhaps the more important message is that many people have confidence in the student and an interest in his or her ultimate success. The therapist may have to help the student understand that this does not represent a burden of unrealistic expectations. "Everyone expects too much of me," students often say. The therapist needs to clarify what the student is hearing. The encouragement needs to be clearly recognized as support for the student to do his or her best — nothing more.

Sometimes a student turns against school as part of adolescence. This rejection of traditional values may be especially fierce if family issues are complex and the family members are intense.

Helping to Restore Hope and Maintain Commitment

Mrs. J lovingly described her fourteen-year-old daughter, Naomi, as a "belligerent little shit." Father, on the other hand, took up for Naomi and felt he could deal constructively with her. His wife felt that he made excuses for the girl and set no limits on her. The competition between mother and daughter for father's attention was clear. Both parents agreed that Naomi's behavior had deteriorated after her bat mitzvah.

At age fourteen, Naomi was experimenting with a wide range of drugs and was doing no schoolwork. She was frequently truant and she was loud, rebellious, and disruptive when present. All efforts at treating her in the home failed and she was sent to boarding school. Her adjustment there was less than perfect. She once called home to express her love for her father. He was gratified and vindicated until the school called to tell him Naomi had been tripping on acid at the time and expressing her undying love to everyone she met.

However, she gradually settled down, graduated and went to college. She was doing mediocre work in college until she decided to apply to law school. She improved her study habits, brought up her grades, and eventually was accepted to law school where she performed at a high level.

We must always remember that, in addition to all its other purposes, school is a wonderful place to make a point.

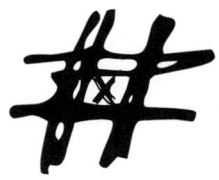

Extra Credit 13

Hope Defined

Hope is the sum of the mental willpower and waypower for goals. Mental willpower is the mental energy and determination that helps move a person in the direction of a goal. Waypower is the mental capacity for a person to be able to find one or more ways or road maps to reach a goal. The following adage applies: "If you can't do it one way, do it another way." Lastly, a goal is simply something a person wants to attain. Goals involving hope fall somewhere in the range of "an impossibility and a sure thing." (based on the work of C.R. Snyder 1994)

Helping to Restore Hope and Maintain Con

Extra Credit 14

Nurturing Hope — Strategies for Parents and Professionals to Enhance Goal Development in Children and Adolescents

- Teach them to use words to specify exactly what they want
- Be certain they consider a few appropriate goals before deciding on one specific goal
- Encourage them to make "stretch goals" (goals more difficult to attain than their previous level of performance)
- Help them select goals that match their skills and strengths Attainable
- Show interest in their goals
- If they have conflicting goals, demonstrate how this could become a problem and help them select one goal
- Direct them to select goals they want as opposed to what others may want for them Set own benchmarks!
- Compliment them when they make good goals for themselves

(based on the work of C.R. Snyder 1994)

THE LEARNING ALLIANCE

Extra Credit 15

Strategies for Parents and Professionals to Enhance Children's and Adolescents' Willpower Thinking

- Make sure they realize they are the ones who make goals become realities
- Help them focus on their strengths and minimize their weaknesses
- Remind them that barriers and roadblocks are part of life and they have to learn to deal with them effectively
- Relate how you successfully and sometimes unsuccessfully coped with your personal barriers and roadblocks when you were a child
- Help them look at barriers and roadblocks as challenges rather than first steps to failure
- Encourage them to laugh at themselves in difficult situations
- Teach them to be patient and learn to wait when they are not getting what they want when they want it

(based on the work of C.R. Snyder 1994)

Helping to Restore Hope and Maintain Commitment

Extra Credit 16

Strategies for Parents and Professionals to Enhance Children's and Adolescents' Waypower

- Listen to their explanations about why some things happen
- Help build their academic, physical, and social skills
- Instruct them to break down goals in smaller, doable steps
- Coach them to think of failures as the use of ineffective strategies rather than their lack of skills or ability
- Have them share their plans for reaching their goals with you

(based on the work of C.R. Snyder 1994)

Leave me alone.

I did all my homework at school.

The Role of the Family
in Academic and Vocational Success

In *People of the Lie*, Scott Peck (1983) says, "If one wants to seek out evil people, the simplest way to do so is to trace them from their victims. The best place to look, then, is among the parents of emotionally disturbed children or adolescents." Although this statement is extreme, it does follow a long tradition of parent bashing in both mental health and education. We have had "momism," the schizophrenogenic mother, the seductive father, the "refrigerator mother," the "double bind," and many other examples of our tendency to blame parents for the problems of their children. There have also been more measured assessments of the psychology of parenting (Markowitz 1975; Parens 1975; Weissman and Cohen 1985) and even some rather positive statements (Robinson 1990). Regardless of the therapist's attitudes, this history of blame has lead parents and guardians to be on the defensive. The intense investment that most parents have in the educational success of their children makes them even more vulnerable to any suggestion that they are to blame for their child's difficulties.

Parents and guardians often feel criticized when they are in-

THE LEARNING ALLIANCE

formed that their child is doing poorly in school even if they are not directly blamed. This is particularly true if the child's behavior is angering school staff. At the same time, the parent is not at all clear about how they can be helpful to school staff. Sometimes parents believe school staff does not understand their child or that the school is not doing enough to help. Sometimes they believe the school is treating their child unfairly. Of course, sometimes they are at least partly correct. Even when they accept the child's responsibility for the difficulty, they wonder, reasonably enough, why the school with all its trained personnel and resources is expecting them to solve their child's academic problems. The sometimes necessary but still regrettable practice of suspending students as a punishment for unacceptable behavior may reinforce this perception. Some may say, "Just when my child needs help the most you dump him back in my lap. What do you expect me to do?"

It is crucial for the school to gain an alliance with the student's family in spite of all these obstacles. Success requires persistence, patience, and some degree of creativity. Occasionally, the job is surprisingly easy. Many parents are astoundingly resilient. After multiple failures and disappointments, they stand ready to try again, somehow holding on to basic confidence in the potential of their child and the skills and good intentions of therapists and educators. They require only the opportunity to cooperate fully with the school. Thank your lucky stars for them.

Other parents are not prepared to be engaged and will need extra effort in order to help them maximize their value to the student in their home. Other students are in foster care or in group homes where parent surrogates vary widely in their commitment to the youngsters in their care. In all cases, however, therapists should never assume there is no home support and should never accept the first hostile or rejecting response they might receive. Podorefsky, McDonald-Dowdell, and Beardsley (2001) have offered valuable guidance regarding an approach to low-income families that has research-supported effectiveness. There are several important steps

The Role of the Family in Academic and Vocational Success

involved in forging a cooperative working relationship with parents and those in loco parentis.

Steps to Successful Parent-School Relationships

Many parents, especially parents of adolescents, do not believe that they are crucially important in their child's life. They do not know that their school involvement is pivotal to the question of whether their child succeeds or fails in school. Since most families with youngsters who have had major school difficulties have some degree of conflict, parents have been told many times by their child that she or he prefers that they have very little to do with his or her life. The students beg parents not to embarrass them by coming to school, are loath to talk about school experiences, and forbid the parent to ask about homework. The parent has often been drawn into angry criticism of the student, draconian punishments, and emotional withdrawal. Parents and guardians, of course, may have their own emotional, addictive, or social problems that limit their flexibility and effectiveness with their children. These tribulations may lower their self-esteem and make it difficult for them to see their importance and potential value to their child. But with or without problems, all parents need to be told repeatedly that they are central in their child's education. They also need to be treated in ways that show them this is the sincere belief of the school. This confidence in the value of the parental contribution to educational success must include a willingness to listen carefully and with an open mind to the suggestions and criticisms the parent may offer regarding the school's policies and procedures as well as the educational techniques used with their child. Of course, this does not mean that school personnel will always agree with parental perceptions, just that they will listen with respect, consider possible changes, and give honest responses regarding which ideas are acceptable and which are not.

This solid foundation supports the later requests for help or suggestions that the parent might alter a behavior that interferes with learning or add a behavior that might help. Convincing parents of their value in school success is crucial to enlisting them in the learning alliance.

The second building block in developing parental support is to establish the school's commitment to understanding *each* child and the school's ability to help *each* child. Both messages are best delivered through well-informed discussions of the student's strengths and areas of vulnerability. Observations about the student are not presented as absolutes and early conclusions are checked with the parent to insure that everyone is in general agreement about goals and techniques. Needless to say, these discussions need to occur as early as possible in the student's school experience and preferably before there has been a major problem. The therapist might say, "I'm glad to have this chance to talk with you. I'm just getting to know Aretta. I'm getting some ideas about why school has been a problem for her but I really need to check them out with you and get any ideas you've had. I'd really like to see us build on her strengths and help her begin to succeed and enjoy school."

In the ensuing discussion it is important to emphasize strengths and to note the youngster's appealing qualities. The parent needs to know that the child is liked and is seen as a valuable addition to the school. Obvious problems such as anger control are mentioned and the need for improvement is openly acknowledged. In fact, this is a good time to inquire about past efforts to help the youngster. Has the youngster had a neurological exam? Has anyone ever recommended medication? Did the child take the medication and did it help or were there side-effects or other problems with the medicine? Does the child show the same temper outbursts at home? How does the parent handle them and what techniques have been helpful? These explorations are not aimed at seeking immediate solutions but are designed to set the scene for possible later interventions and to anchor future interventions within an overall understanding of the student.

The emphasis remains on how the problem, whatever it may be, affects the learning process. The questions and observations are all part of a school evaluation and that focus is kept clearly in mind. This

The Role of the Family in Academic and Vocational Success

will be helpful if it becomes necessary at some point to ask *personal* questions of the parents. Such matters would be none of our business except that they may influence the child's educational progress.

Occasionally, you may encounter a parent who views your understanding as ignorance. They believe you have been conned by their child. The strengths you purport to see in the child are actually clever pretensions with which this youngster regularly fools adults. You have been taken in and do not realize how bad this little demon actually is. When confronted with this reaction the therapist should always recall there are two possibilities. The most common explanation, by far, is that you are dealing with a parent who has come to totally reject her child. These parents do not want to hear that the kid has any redeeming merit. In these instances one must back off, thank the parent for the heads up, and promise that all the staff will be warned to be alert for trickery. These parents will be won over only by an extended period of positive performance from the child that wins back their trust. The therapist can be frank with the student about the need to prove themselves and the wisdom of avoiding lies and deceit in their family dealings. It is almost always a mistake to try to sell these students back to their parents prematurely since that only reinforces the opinion that you are a softhearted sucker. On the other hand, one does not have to agree with the parent's suspicion. It is useful to say, "We haven't seen that kind of manipulation here as yet but after what you have told me we will certainly keep our eyes wide open." If the student continues to do well a later report to the parent might go as far as to suggest tentatively that the student might have turned over a new leaf since he or she has been "pretty honest and straightforward" so far.

> *Shauna's mother was outraged that the school district placed her daughter in a special education day program. The seventeen-year-old junior had failed two consecutive school years because of flagrant acting out, including drug use, delinquent activity, and frequent runaway behavior. Her*

THE LEARNING ALLIANCE

> *mother had expected residential placement, partly because her patience and coping abilities were at their limit.*
>
> *The mother became even angrier when the school's evaluation and Shauna's adjustment suggested that the outpatient placement could succeed. The mother felt that Shauna had definitely outsmarted the school staff. After a semester of success, however, the mother became gradually and somewhat reluctantly cooperative with the program. This alliance even weathered several major setbacks in Shauna's progress and contributed mightily to her eventual rather spectacular success.*

We did say there were two possibilities. The other is that the student may have major sociopathic defenses and you may have been conned by a pro. If so, that will become obvious over time. It is much better to be too trusting and optimistic than to constantly expect the worst.

Awareness of School Policies and Procedures

It is essential to educate the parent regarding the school's policies and procedures by explaining their importance and necessity in furthering the education of students. Physical restraint, use of isolation or *quiet* rooms, suspension, drug testing, and even dress codes can be controversial to some parents. Although these policies are not negotiable and must apply equally to all students, it is important to allow for open discussion and even disagreement. The therapist can patiently explain the concepts and intentions behind each rule without arguing with the parent or trying actively to change their mind. If the parent offers ideas or new ways of looking at an issue or policy, the therapist should express appreciation and indicate that the ideas will be presented to the school staff for consideration. At the same time the therapist, as a representative of the school, should quietly but firmly make it clear that there are no immediate plans to change the rules because they are believed to be in the best interests of the educational process and the well-

The Role of the Family in Academic and Vocational Success

being of all the students. If changes are to come they will appear only after the staff and the school leadership have considered them carefully. In the meantime, the school needs parental support for the expectation that the student will follow the rules; even those the parent is questioning.

Using the Individualized Educational Plan as a Guide

At the level of the individual student, the therapist and the parent need to be <u>aware of the specific goals for each student</u>, usually spelled out in the student's Individualized Education Program (IEP). The IEP is developed by the IEP Team, which includes the student and the parent/guardian, special education teacher, therapist, administrators, representatives from the student's local school system, and related professionals. The therapist, along with administrators and special education teachers, must share responsibility for making sure the IEP is presented to the student and parent clearly and without jargon. Once the design of the IEP is completed and participants' signatures are affixed, the student's home school system, teachers, therapists, administrators, and the parent should be given a copy of the IEP.

The early review of the IEP is the first opportunity to discuss the parent's role in achieving IEP goals. It is often wise to begin by asking how the parent has addressed the pertinent issues in the past and to inquire about the student's response. This discussion may reveal that some past approaches were effective but were abandoned because the problem seemed to be resolved or because the parent was distracted by other events. Past failures can be equally illuminating and can suggest avenues that probably should be avoided. If the discussion reveals major areas of difficulty such as parental inability to set limits, the therapist can begin to explore the reasons behind the faulty parent-child interaction.

As a rule, especially at schools designed to educate children with emotional problems, the referral packet will include a social history that can shed light on important factors that may require attention. At the same time these social histories can be overwhelming

THE LEARNING ALLIANCE

and even counter-productive. Many families of students with emotional difficulties have had major traumas and dislocations. Condensing all these tribulations on a few pages can have the effect of obscuring family strengths and suggesting that the situation is hopeless. The therapist should remember that they do not have the task of solving all problems and righting all wrongs. The focus should be on mobilizing parental resources and using them selectively to augment the student's effort to get an education. Many parents have neither the time nor the inclination to attend regular formal therapy sessions. Much work has to be done on the telephone and during emergency meetings that include the student. A clear agenda established early in the school experience and a plan containing a few achievable goals is superior to extensive, unrealizable, and ultimately frustrating grandiose treatment plans. This is not to say that family treatment is never indicated. In some cases, family therapy is crucial in helping the student and family get back on track. Often this will have to be provided outside of school, for example in the evening near the student's home.

Offering Effective Techniques for Parents and Guardians

As the therapist-parent relationship becomes stronger the therapist may be able to offer suggestions regarding more effective techniques that the parents can use in their efforts to mentor, monitor, and inspire their child. These suggestions will be more easily accepted if they can be tied to previous approaches that have worked for the parent. For example, the therapist might say, "You know, I remember that you told me Jackson responds better to friendly discussions about school than he does to strict rules about homework times. Do you think you should go back to that approach?" Or the therapist might say, "I really think Jackson is not so much lazy right now as discouraged. In the past didn't he often get going again when you gave him a lot of praise and credit for the good things he does?"

On the other hand, there are times when we need to say, "Right now I'm afraid that Jackson is just trying to ignore and avoid the problem. Would you be comfortable to increase the structure at

The Role of the Family in Academic and Vocational Success

home? I'm thinking of something like you requiring him to bring home weekly progress notes and tying these to some of his fun activities like TV or computer time? How would you feel about that?"

On the same general theme, the school and the therapist need to provide many opportunities for the students to demonstrate their skills and accomplishments to their parents. It is not only the child or adolescent that is starved for positive feedback. The parents too are hungry for encouraging information about their children. Art exhibits, behavioral improvements, written work, and musical performances offer possibilities to showcase student achievements.

Therapists cannot share this kind of good news unless they know it. Too often, school staff meetings are dominated by dramatic negative events and current upsets. It is very important for both parent and school staff morale, for therapists to save time to report on the constructive work that is accomplished in the midst of the chaos.

Many therapists will read these paragraphs with envy since a large proportion of the students assigned to them will have only parental surrogates in their lives. Biological parents may be drug addicted, incarcerated, or otherwise unavailable. Sometimes, even worse, they are only sporadically available, holding out promises to the youngsters that build hopes doomed to be crushed by the parent's unreliability.

Still other parents are available but are truly unfit to parent. For example, the parent may use drugs with the child or share other illegal activities while actively undermining academic and vocational ambitions. These situations are very trying to the therapist and may lead to a sense of futility. However, if the child continues to attend school and to speak in therapy sessions, then that is strong evidence of an abiding, if threatened, acceptance of positive life goals. A cautionary statement is important here. No matter how toxic a parent may seem to the therapist it is almost always counterproductive to criticize the parent to the student. Youngsters have a strong need to defend their parents to others. Often they prefer to blame themselves for parental shortcomings.

THE LEARNING ALLIANCE

Hector's mother was a severe heroin addict. She had no interest in Hector's activities or thoughts. She was somewhat more engaged with his younger sister for the simple reason that the girl was "parentified" and often cared for the mother. Still, Hector broke down in therapy one day and wept while vilifying himself for his inability to win his mother's approval.

Even when the child criticizes the parent it is wise to accept the feelings without joining in the judgment. In fact, it is often wise to voice some understanding for the parent. "It really is unfortunate that your mother couldn't help you more in growing up. Drugs sometimes keep people from being able to do the things they would like to do." This is best for two reasons. First of all, almost all children retain some love for their parents no matter how destructive the parent may have been. Secondly, even when rage at the parent has overcome any ambivalence, the young person will still need to understand if not forgive. If this never occurs, the parent is demonized and occupies great power in the youngster's life forever.

Nonbiological Parenting

Children and adolescents in foster care appear to be at high risk for emotional or behavioral problems and school-related problems (Smucker et al. 1996). Rarely are children or adolescents placed in substitute care unless they have suffered some sort of trauma that is likely to result in at least short-term emotional problems.

Foster parents present entirely different issues. Some foster parents have cared for the student for years and have shown their devotion by remaining loyal and steadfast through rough times. They are the child's true emotional parents. Adoptive parents have taken their commitment a step further and have legalized their parental role. However, the situation is complicated in both cases by the fact that one set of parents abandoned the child in the past. Often some of the intense feelings related to that critical fact are unfairly attached to the new caretakers. Foster children and foster parents face

The Role of the Family in Academic and Vocational Success

many stresses. A major problem in providing foster care is finding caregivers who are highly skilled in child rearing (Moore and Chamberlain 1994). Many foster parents receive little or no training and few are skilled enough to deal with children or adolescents with emotional or behavioral problems.

Foster parents may be recent entrants in the child's life. Some students have been through multiple placements and view their current house as a temporary stopping point. The risk for negative emotional or behavioral problems appears to increase with the number of placements (Smucker et al. 1996). The lack of nurturing, continuity, stability, and attachment that goes with numerous placements is highly likely to cause emotional or behavioral problems (Clark et al. 1994). Every therapist needs to study and understand the special issues these families bring.

Group home staff members have many children in their care and may be more tuned to their group management responsibilities than to the needs of any single child. When no one is truly and clearly in the parental role in a student's life it may fall to the therapist to try to find a substitute. Mentoring programs such as Big Brothers, some churches, and community outreach programs may be helpful. To a limited extent the therapist may be chosen by the student to assume a parenting role. It is not unusual for this wish to be expressed quite directly; the student may plead with the therapist to adopt them. These understandable wishes have to be handled delicately. It is unwise and ultimately destructive to give in to this wish, even partially. Even if the therapist was prepared to adopt a child, the granting of what is basically a transference wish is fraught with peril. The student may be led to believe that wishes do come true, which may interfere with the development of a reality sense. This will make the crushing disappointment more severe when the idealized therapist has to take on the more mundane, sometimes frustrating and ambivalently perceived parental role. Rescue fantasies are understandable. Real life efforts to rescue often end badly.

This is not to say that there are no legitimate parenting roles for therapists. Probably most child and adolescent clients experience

THE LEARNING ALLIANCE

their therapists as parental objects to some extent. A similar process occurs with teachers. Many graduated students, especially those without other close family members, come back to visit their schools so that teachers and therapists can hear of their successes and marvel at how wonderful they look. These occurrences surely do feel like a visit home!

> *After Hector had an emotional catharsis regarding his failure to earn his mother's love, his therapist made the following intervention.*
>
> *"I'm not sure why you and your mother aren't closer. I don't really know her. I can only say that if you were my son, I would notice that you attend school every day and make good grades while holding down a job and that you have a million friends. I would be very proud of you."*

Are teachers soul savers?

7

Collaboration
between Therapists and Teachers

This chapter is based on a statement made to one of the authors some years ago. The speaker was the superintendent of a large school district who was being asked to assign teachers to a school program opening in a local psychiatric hospital. The superintendent said that he would ask for volunteers but he doubted that any would come forward. "Teachers," he explained, "aren't interested in being soul savers."

"Do they see themselves as mind savers?" one of the authors asked.

The superintendent nodded. "Yes, you could say that."

As a matter of fact, several teachers jumped at the chance to teach students with emotional disturbance in collaboration with mental health workers. Still, the superintendent's distinction has some merit. This chapter focuses on the conflicts that teachers and therapists sometimes have with one another due to their differing perspectives and goals for students. The notion that teachers are more rigid and punitive — the term *custodial* is sometimes used in the literature — while therapists are more understanding, flexible, and hu-

THE LEARNING ALLIANCE

manistic is held by some mental health professionals. When mental health professionals address educators, they often sound critical and perhaps a bit condescending. In the prologue to *Freedom to Learn* (1969) Carl Rogers says, "I am writing this book because I want to speak to teachers, professors, educators, administrators of schools, colleges, and educational institutions. I want to speak to them about *learning*. But *not* the lifeless, sterile, futile, quickly forgotten stuff which is crammed into the mind of the poor helpless individual tied into his seat by ironbound bonds of conformity!" Not exactly a ringing endorsement of basic education!

Therapists and Teachers are Different and Think Differently!

Before we rush to protect our students from these folk who would hobble them with bonds of rigid conformity, we therapists need to recognize that we begin with certain advantages in the endeavor to understand the complex reasons behind the behavior of troubled students. To begin with, there is a basic difference in numbers. A therapist working in a special education program is typically responsible for twelve to sixteen students. An elementary school teacher in a special education program may have a comparable student assignment, but middle school and high school teachers, even with the lower class size of a special education school have to get to know forty to sixty youngsters as they rotate through their classes. In addition, the teacher's time is more structured, allowing less opportunity for phone calls and other informal contacts. These differences mean that therapists have an earlier and slightly more relaxed opportunity to get to know new students and their families in some depth. In addition, although special education training programs usually offer some instruction in psychopathology to teachers, it is minimal compared to the learning opportunities that mental health trainees are offered in that area. Teachers' training must include curriculum planning, class management, academic assessment, teaching methodology, legal issues, and other educational specialties so there is limited available time for emotional dynamics, psychiatric diagnosis, and clinical presentation. Thera-

Collaboration between Therapists and Teachers

pists have the requisite background and carry the primary responsibility for helping teachers and other school staff to understand each child's psychic makeup.

A related time factor in the differing understanding that each profession brings to the student is the greater amount of individual contact that therapists have with students in most programs. Teachers encounter students primarily in the group setting of the classroom. Students are much more likely to be attentive to their *image* in the company of their peers. This may make it difficult for them to be self-revealing. Similar issues arise in group therapy but confidentiality and the model provided by more trusting, therapy-ready youngsters may encourage emotional honesty in those settings. The classroom, on the other hand, is very public and geared toward gaining information and skills, not toward personal declarations. Sometimes the overall result is that the teacher has less opportunity to see behind the camouflage and into the student's hidden pain. Although therapists must also expect the student to master their demons and improve his or her behavior it may be easier for them to forgive temporary setbacks since they have more opportunity to understand the source.

Different Roles in the Collaboration Process

Therapists not only have more opportunity and time to understand the student in depth, they also do not have to demand performance from the student on a daily basis. It is the task of the teacher to strongly encourage academic effort each and every day. To grant the student permission to completely forget schoolwork because of upset feelings is not in the student's best interest. In the real world one must learn to compartmentalize conflict and personal concerns and somehow remain at least partly productive. To fail to do so over any extended period can be disastrous to one's welfare. This is one of several ways that the classroom resembles the outside world more closely than does the psychological consulting room.

Therapists may welcome the open exhibition of the student's emotional pathology since problems then become evident and

THE LEARNING ALLIANCE

available to therapy. Teachers on the other hand have the responsibility to maintain a learning atmosphere in the classroom. Disruptions of any kind are a problem. Even very understanding teachers have to ask the student to take up these individual issues with his or her therapist — not in the middle of learning algebra. The teacher's need to press for performance and production even when the student is in psychological distress may conflict with the therapist's wish to nurture and comfort the troubled student. The teacher's involvement with the student is often more difficult since contacts are usually in a group setting and many students with academic disabilities use the group to divert attention from their learning problems — often at the expense of classroom decorum and the teacher's class goals. To some extent the teacher's first priority is a classroom atmosphere conducive to learning — a group goal only reluctantly sacrificed to the needs of the individual student. On the other hand, the therapist — though sympathetic to group needs — has a major responsibility for the well-being of the individual student. These views can create a situation where the therapist views the teacher as an unfeeling pedagogue while the teacher believes the therapist is coddling the students. It is important for therapists to remember that, while they work to provide the mortar that allows a child to build his life, teachers are struggling to provide the bricks. It is obvious that both provide essential nurture.

Successful collaboration between the professions starts with a basic understanding of the points above, is nourished by mutual respect, and grows through open communication. Teachers can certainly be blinded by counter-transference just as therapists can (Millington and Malloy 1988). Therapists can set an example of comfortable self-scrutiny and guide other staff to open exploration of our emotional responses to students. This is never easy but it is an essential element in maintaining a truly therapeutic school. Most school programs provide a forum for multidisciplinary interaction where this kind of tough work can be tackled. These meetings need to include not only problem-solving opportunities but also mutual

Collaboration between Therapists and Teachers

support and recognition. The interdependence of all staff needs to be plainly acknowledged at every opportunity.

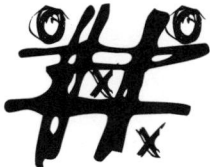

THE LEARNING ALLIANCE

Extra Credit 17

Ideas for Collaboration between Therapists and Teachers

- Meet to clarify role expectations at the beginning of the school year
- Obtain copies of teachers' syllabi for the semester or year to familiarize yourself with content of student work, topics, subjects, etc.
- Schedule regular meetings with teachers of students on caseload
- Co-teach a social skills class with a teacher in her/his classroom
- Consult with teachers regularly and meet to identify problems and develop meaningful interventions
- Plan with the teachers to visit the classrooms of the students on caseload
- Invite teachers to present a topic during group therapy time
- Review academic, behavioral, and social-emotional progress on a regular basis with teachers
- Seek out opportunities that will promote an integrated approach in meeting the needs of each individual student
- Meet with parents/guardians as a team

Collaboration between Therapists and Teachers

Extra Credit 18
Therapist Standards and Expectations

Purpose:
To provide individual therapy and case management services to help students with emotional disturbance regain their ability to function in school.
To achieve this purpose, therapists are expected to:
- Function as a liaison for the students among interdisciplinary team members within the school and involved parties outside of the school.
- Advocate throughout the day for students in their attempts to be more successful in school.
- Develop and maintain appropriate professional boundaries and positive professional relationships with students, staff, parents and guardians.
- Develop a working knowledge of support services available within the community.
- Develop good relationships with the individuals who represent these community resources.
- Complete required documentation within stated timelines including weekly progress notes and documentation of all contacts with parents, guardians and outside agencies.
- Support student progress through the effective management of appropriate therapeutic medication if prescribed.
- Maintain state of the art clinical skills through professional development opportunities.

continued on following page…

THE LEARNING ALLIANCE

...*continued from previous page*
- Provide individual therapy in compliance with the IEP and making up all missed sessions within one week.
- Schedule weekly individual therapy as assigned by the clinical director as well as provide a weekly schedule of individual therapy sessions.
- Contact the teacher in advance regarding any changes in the schedule of therapy sessions.
- Document all individual and group therapy sessions and submit copies for each student's record.

Supervision:
Your ability to meet these expectations and standards will be reflected in your daily performance. Supervision will be the forum for assessing your performance and supporting your growth.

(Kaler, Sacclaris, and Weddington-Ruhl 2000)

Collaboration between Therapists and Teachers

Extra Credit 19
Teacher Standards and Expectations

Purpose:
To develop a consistent standard of operation in classrooms that will promote success for students and build positive relationships with colleagues and parents/guardians.

To achieve this stated purpose, teachers are expected to:
- Establish and maintain a classroom environment that encourages learning and reflects organization, creativity and professionalism.
- Clearly define classroom procedures and expectations.
- Provide an adequate amount of classwork for every student throughout each class period.
- Assign tasks to students that are suited to their performance level and sufficiently challenging.
- Respond to student behavior in accordance with classroom behavioral criteria and the overall school behavior management system.
- Use available resources both inside and outside the school to maximize learning opportunities.
- Provide adequate substitute plans in writing for all classroom coverage needs.
- Complete and submit all required documentation within stated timelines.
- Actively participate in the facilitation of the therapeutic process in the weekly community meeting.
- Maintain professional boundaries in all interactions with students, parents/guardians and staff.

continued on following page…

THE LEARNING ALLIANCE

...*continued from previous page*
- Communicate with parents/guardians in a consistent and timely manner regarding all aspects of the student's academic performance and classroom behavior.
- Document all phone contacts made to parents/guardians.
- Exhibit professional conduct when participating in all meetings.
- Be well prepared for all professional meetings.
- Develop and maintain professional skills through educational and training opportunities.

(Kaler, Sacclaris, and Weddington-Ruhl 2000)

What's the big hassle?

I'm cool.

Drug Use
and Academic Work

Youngsters with behavioral disorders are about four times more likely to show patterns of heavy drug use than are nondisordered children and adolescents (Kress and Elias, 1993). Most students referred for special education have the same risk factors and the incidence of damaging drug usage is very high in these programs. These facts indicate a strong need for both prevention and treatment programs in special education. Active drug education, appropriate skill training, and attention to depression and other risk factors should begin in the earliest grades and continue as the child advances through the school experience. Treatment of heavy drug use, once it is clearly established, is difficult and expensive. Time and resources directed toward prevention are well spent. This statement would hold true in *any* school. The value of prevention programs has been well documented although they do not always lead to sobriety (Eggert et al. 1992; Harrell 1996; Thompson et al.1997).

Elements of School-based Drug Prevention and Treatment
There are multiple elements to school-based drug prevention and

treatment programs. Let's start with attendance. Someone once said, "Showing up is 90 percent of the secret of success." He could well have been talking about education. In tracking more than a hundred special education high school students enrolled in The Foundation Schools, the best predictor of grade point average was attendance. In turn, the best inverse predictor of attendance was drug use. One can't be sure which is the chicken and which is the egg: Do people who forsake the structure of school become more vulnerable to drug use or does drug use breed neglect of school duties? In any case, the two problems occur together and need to be addressed simultaneously. Before you can help the student, you must find the student. The school cannot involve an absent student in even the finest school-based program. A community connection that can reach out to the truant student is essential. For many special education schools, the expense involved in reducing drug use may be considered prohibitive. Too often the problem is just ignored. For example, an informal survey of programs for students with emotional disturbance in the Washington, D.C., metropolitan area showed that only about a third provided drug testing, a basic starting point for monitoring drug usage. Hiring trained drug counselors, providing regular drug counseling sessions, and communicating with the families of students in treatment is costly and is often not considered an educational expense. This policy may be short sighted in view of the proven impact of drug use on cognitive and behavioral performance (Budney et al. 2001; Reneman et al. 2001; Pope et.al. 2001) Even schools that try to screen out drug involved students still have many active drug users busily undermining their educational efforts. Many of our students are attracted to what Stanton and Todd (1982) dubbed *pseudo-individuation* as drug use allows a surface appearance of spirited independence while creating enough dysfunction to insure continuing dependence.

Creating a Drug-free School Environment
If a school decides to make a serious effort to create a drug-free environment, the first step should be directed toward gaining staff and

Drug Use and Academic Work

student support. This is a daunting task. In elementary schools some students will verbally endorse drug use even if they don't actually indulge. For them a knowing attitude toward drug use may seem cool and more grown up. In addition, for many of them, their blasé attitude reflects the broad acceptance of drug use in society and in their home community. This is not to say that younger students do not get involved with drugs. If the student's family or community allows easy access to drugs and little supervision, drug use can appear very early in life. Adolescents with serious drug problems often report that their usage began at eight to ten years of age, sometimes even earlier. Elementary grade children who defend drug use should be taken seriously and evaluated for present or future risks. At the minimum they deserve drug prevention education and training in the social skills that might help them avoid being drawn into the drug scene.

In middle school and senior high the situation is even more complicated. Some older students are reluctant to voice opinions opposing drug use because they don't wish to criticize their friends — particularly since most of them have experimented with drugs at least once themselves. They also don't want to be viewed as currying favor with the staff by mouthing the party line. No spunky adolescent wants to look like a shill for adults. A great deal of effort and thought needs to go into drug education approaches if they are to have any credence with adolescents. Efforts to instill fear of drug use are likely to fail. Adolescents are usually personally acquainted with someone who uses drugs without any apparent negative effects. In addition, adolescents are by nature fearless, at least they often have a counter-phobic response to adult warnings! Even if they accept the idea that some people are damaged by drugs, they believe themselves to be smarter and stronger. They say of the victims, "They were stupid. They let it get out of hand. I would never do that." These students respond better to factual studies that report subtle negative effects in a measured, scientific manner. The data supporting drug interference with the learning process is impressive (Reneman et al. 2001; Pope et al. 2001: Budney et al. 2001).

THE LEARNING ALLIANCE

One needs to be ready to answer the student objection that some honor students are active drug users. The answer, of course, is that superior students have capacity to spare but would probably be even more effective without drugs. In addition, students may be reminded that negative effects are incremental with continuing drug use. Information about risk factors for addictions, including family history and usage patterns, are usually accepted by young people without major disagreement. Recovering addicts can be very helpful in reaching students in denial. They are usually glad to describe their experiences since that is often part of their own rehabilitation in their twelve-step program. Many of them began their drugging in adolescence and they often describe patterns of denial and justification identical to those currently being used by their audience.

Organizing essay and poster contests pointing out the reasons to avoid drug involvement can be helpful. Once the adolescent makes a creative, personal statement of opposition, which is based on his or her own reasons, it becomes easier for him or her to adopt an anti-drug stance. Group discussions that focus not on the adolescent's direct experience with drugs but on ways that drugs and alcohol have damaged family or friends can be powerful reminders of the serious downside of drug involvement. This approach also allows a nonthreatening opportunity to assess the adolescent's exposure to drug use and her knowledge and sophistication in that area. Another ancillary gain is the chance to address COCD (children of the chemically dependent) issues, those subtle and enduring wounds that result from growing up in a family distorted by drug addiction. These problems are common in children with educational difficulties. Naturally, all these approaches must be repeated creatively in a sustained but thoughtful effort to elicit student support for a drug-free school environment.

Gaining genuine and sincere staff support for a drug-free school is sometimes more difficult than one might assume. Those staff members who have had no direct training in addiction often are simply unaware there is a problem. They tend to be taken in by the students' denial of drug use and may even be unaware that one of

Drug Use and Academic Work

their students is behaving strangely because of intoxication. These lapses are simply due to inadequate training and a resulting lack of sensitivity to the issue. It may be particularly difficult to confront a student who is vociferously denying drug use unless one is well armed by training and experience. It is always tempting to avoid talking about charged topics. One sees this in the tragic failure to actively pursue suicidal or homicidal hints, but it is even more evident when staff have to talk about dirty deeds like drug use, involvement in gangs, or prostitution. These all come from another world where nice people are reluctant to visit.

There are other, more subtle, reasons why staff may be lackadaisical in their support of a drug-free school. One factor is the general cultural acceptance of drug use as a normative behavior. Television and movies suggest that alcohol and drug usage is commonplace. Professional athletes and media stars are widely publicized as drug users — often without extensive attention to those whose careers are seriously damaged or destroyed in that way. Even more important is the fact that the staff is a microcosm of the wider society so that there will be several staff members who use drugs themselves. If the staff is large it will likely contain one or more people who are drug dependent or afraid they are approaching that condition. They may have strong reasons to avoid thinking seriously about drugs. Fortunately most staff who use drugs will be social drinkers. Some will use marijuana in moderation. Those staff members are often reluctant to oppose drug use in a strong and open way because they don't want to be hypocritical or to lie if students challenge them about their own behavior. Often it is necessary to help them understand that opposing drug use for students is not a moral stance. Staff members should be trained to avoid extensive discussions of their own drug use — past or present. The staff member is not on trial and is not judging the student or condemning evil actions. The staff member merely is stating a strong opinion that the student would be wise to avoid drug use while pursuing an education. Students with school problems already are struggling with multiple risk factors. They don't need still another. This is an adequate position to support the school's basic message. Those students who already have an active drug problem will need to understand the wider corrosive impact of heavy drug use on every aspect of their lives. This is a job for specially trained counselors.

Identifying Students with Chemical Dependency Problems

This leads us to the next element of an effective program to address the drug problem in schools. Those students with serious involvement in the drug scene must be identified so that they can receive proper treatment. The diagnosis of drug problems begins with the initial admission evaluation. A careful history may discover clear evidence of a problem. Even when there has been no official diagnosis the family may reveal concerns or the student may describe conflict with the parents about drugs. Sometimes indirect questions may give hints. For example, one can ask about the extent of drug use in schools the student has attended and about the extent of usage among friends and family. Often the drug-involved youngster exaggerates the prevalence of drug involvement in others, saying, "Man, everybody at that school smoked and lots of them were dealing — I mean the smart kids, the jocks, everyone! The principal didn't have a clue." On the other hand, if one asks about drug use among the student's close personal friends, these young people seem to be the exception. "Oh no, the guys that I run with don't have time for that stuff."

Occasionally the drug-using student will admit to past drug use and deny usage in the present. One can learn a great deal by accepting the evasion and encouraging extensive discussion of past patterns of drug use and attitudes toward drugs' effects. Paradoxically it can be very useful to discuss the student's positive reactions to drug use. One can ask, "How did they make you feel?" After all, if there were no benefits the drugs would not have been desired — then or now. Matter-of-fact questions about how the student first learned about drugs and who provided his first drugs can provide important information regarding motivations and patterns of use.

Drug Use and Academic Work

The Impact of Chemical Dependency

Eventually one wants to explore the negative impacts of drug use. Were there family fights over drugs or parental concerns about friends? Extreme changes in the relationship between the student and other family members, usually toward withdrawal and hostility, often are the results of drug usage. The drug-using student feels guilt and often tries to provoke parents into behavior that would justify jettisoning the values the parents have taught. Talking about friends can sometimes be informative in other ways. Dropping old friends for a new group often happens because the youngster becomes involved with drugs and gravitates toward other users. Often the student is secretive about these new friends and may be reluctant for the parents to meet them or get to know them. Careful attention should be given to geographic moves during the student's adolescence. Losing a peer network and established social position during this developmental period can lead to anxiety, depression, and loneliness. It can be difficult to break into an established peer hierarchy in the new school setting. On the other hand, drug-involved youngsters welcome newcomers to their group if the person is willing to use. The new student is an appreciated partner in crime, sharing in the guilt and providing a new profit center. You don't have to be pretty or smart to be accepted by the users. Even if you are but you find the new social setting to be competitive and snotty, you can gain apparent loving acceptance just by joining the drug group. Only much later, if ever, the adolescent will realize that *drugships* (Chambers 1999) are not really friendships. In friendship, the person is important, in drugships, things — the drugs — are central. The point for the examiner is that one should listen carefully for changes in a student's peer group.

It is also worth exploring changes in leisure activities and interests. When youngsters become involved with drugs they often drop more wholesome activities. Athletics, musical performance, dance, and other hobbies that require application and skill development are often abandoned. Changes in energy, sleep patterns, styles of dress, and self-care may also give clues about possible drug involvement. A useful question is: "Over the years have you found yourself changing? Tell me about the changes, especially any that were really important to you." Many drug-involved youngsters will describe changes but say that the new patterns represent their true selves, while earlier, better adjusted personas were fake. They may explain that they were only trying to please others, especially parents.

Part of the defense of denial is the reluctance to believe or to admit to oneself or others that drugs have created problems. It often takes careful and persistent interviewing to establish the fact that the student's academic performance deteriorated once drug use began. Sometimes the student will acknowledge the poor performance, but blame it on parents, teachers, or others. Even if the drug use led to legal charges, the student may maintain that the charges were unjustified. One should still collect the facts. Often, at a later date when the student is ready to address the problem honestly, the facts are useful.

There is no substitute for experience in the evaluation of drug abuse. Youngsters with serious drug problems can present themselves as strangers to the drug scene while other students exaggerate their sophistication about drugs in order to appear cool. Only careful interviewing and continued observation of behavior can reveal the truth. Routine and regular drug testing is obviously an aid to this assessment but cannot replace experienced clinical judgement.

Once the group of students with active clinical drug problems has been identified it is necessary to construct an effective drug treatment program to assist them. The intricacies of treating drug dependency are beyond the scope of this chapter but you may find the general outline of successful intervention programs to be useful.

Most observers agree that effective treatment usually involves specialized group therapy coupled with the basic concepts involved in Alcoholics Anonymous, Narcotics Anonymous, and other twelve-step programs. These basics include the honest admission of a drug problem, accepting the fact that complete sobriety is the ideal goal, and the belief that addiction is a disease. These principles have been challenged (Jellinek 1960; Fingarette 1988) and

Drug Use and Academic Work

probably should not be canonized and applied with messianic rigidity, but they are time tested and provide the best general guidelines for treatment. They serve well as long as one remembers that not all adolescents who are heavy drug users are actually addicted (Director 2000)and that many students from drug infested communities or homes do not achieve sobriety in treatment but are able to reduce their usage, attend school more regularly, and perform better academically. Counselors who are themselves recovering addicts can be very effective therapists since they know well the subterfuges as well as the hazards involved in drug dependency. Still the main qualification for therapists is adequate training in the special needs of these students. Even recovering counselors may have major countertransference issues at times, especially around necessary coercive steps, such as involving parents or police or insisting on forced hospitalization. These events may stir negative personal memories of times when others were trying to force them to quit drugs. Everyone needs training, peer support, and active supervision to stay on target in this work.

Individual evaluation and counseling have value in drug treatment but most experts agree that group therapy has many advantages with this population. The mutual support, knowledgeable confrontation, and drug-free socialization are all important. The group experience also reinforces the comradeship of the twelve-step programs. Since few schools can provide all the needed elements of drug treatment, close collaboration with community programs is essential.

Outpatient drug treatment programs also require the availability of inpatient or residential drug treatment. Some of the seriously dependent students simply cannot take the initial steps toward sobriety without supervision and containment on a twenty-four hour basis. Again, collaboration is crucial to insure that an adequate follow-up program is in place after discharge from residential care.

> *Laura was a sixteen-year-old high school junior with many symptoms of a problem development. She was described as*

THE LEARNING ALLIANCE

a hypersensitive infant and toddler who was intolerant of loud noises, new clothes, or bright lights. She was impulsive and difficult to comfort. In elementary school she was diagnosed as learning disabled. She was intensely hostile to both parents, especially her mother. Mother, perhaps understandably, favored a younger sister who was more docile and rewarding. There was a strong family history of severe alcoholism and by age sixteen, Laura was also severely alcoholic.

In therapy Laura admitted her alcohol abuse and expressed her to stop drinking but felt she could not. She also wished for a happier home life.

The therapist recommended that the parents place Laura in a residential drug treatment program but mother refused. She was sure Laura would fight the recommendation and that this uproar would upset the younger sister.

Laura was soon arrested for drunkenness and ordered to A.A. Soon after she got drunk again and had a major suicidal overdose, which finally led to the residential treatment that she needed. Laura was well aware that she could not achieve Inspiration *in the face of her drug use but she could not stop drinking without external controls.*

All students involved in a drug treatment program require long-term support and continuing evaluation. Drug dependency is a chronic condition and relapse is common. Once the drug-involved youngster has a period of sobriety and improved functioning, he or she is likely to decide it is now safe to use drugs socially. Unfortunately, when that proves untrue the student may be demoralized and may view the relapse as proof that he is hopelessly addicted. Realistic counseling, strong support, and crisis intervention are essential at this time to avoid desperate self-destructive actions, such as dropping out of school or even suicidal thoughts. On the other hand, if properly treated, the relapse offers an unsurpassed opportunity for personal growth and greater mastery of the habit.

Drug Use and Academic Work

A Family Dis-ease

The effective drug treatment program recognizes that drug dependency is a family disease and that the student's family includes the school staff. Parents and/or staff may be caught up in the problem. Denying the seriousness of the problem, protecting the student from the consequences of their behavior, and even colluding with drug usage are examples of enabling. All are destructive to the student's progress. The school may be somewhat limited in resources to provide total treatment to the family aside from recognition of the problem; recommendations for community treatment and direct confrontation by involved staff members can often have a considerable impact.

The school also has a responsibility to students who are not drug dependent. Basic drug education should be part of any school curriculum. In addition, most schools will have a group of students who are not seriously drug involved but who are either severely impacted by the drug use of others or at serious risk for drug involvement later. The initial history and evaluation will identify many of these students. Others will reveal themselves through preoccupation with drugs, unusual familiarity with drug terminology, or with revelations of family drug use. These individuals are greatly benefited by the pro-sobriety bias of the school program. They also benefit from prevention programs that include incentives for maintaining and supporting the drug-free philosophy of the school, such as essay contests, poster contests, and public recognition of clean urine tests and other evidences of sobriety.

Extra Credit 20

Stages of Adolescent Substance Abuse

Stage	Experimentation	Active Use	Abuse	Dependency
Description	Occasional use of drugs and/or alcohol usually on weekends or over summer breaks; unplanned use; low tolerance	Start to actively seek social situations where alcohol and/or drugs can be found; changes in peer group; tolerance increases	Getting high becomes preoccupation; start to experience some loss of control; "I don't care" attitude; failure to succeed; attempts to "cut-back"	Preoccupation with getting high totally controls life; very high tolerance; need to use to feel normal; shame and guilt regarding inability to stop; strong defensiveness
Problems	Peer pressure, alcohol poisoning, binge drinking	Peer acceptance, decrease in performance at school, mood changes, hangovers	Self-medication; school failure; attendance problems; experimentation with harder drugs; accidental overdose	Loss of significant relationships; school withdrawal; inability to hold job; hit bottom

(Kunert and Marnell 2002)

Extra Credit 21

Another Path Program Tracks

Drug Use and Academic Work

Prevention Track	Education Track	Treatment Track
• Random Drug Screens • Sobriety Checks • Drug Awareness Week • Schoolwide Speakers/Assemblies • Schoolwide Field Trips • CD Consultations (Ideation) • Staff T-Shirt Day • Bumper Stickers • Banner • Middle School CD Prevention Class • Negative Drug Screen Celebrations • At-Risk Groups	• CD Assessments • Curriculum-based CD Classes • Educational Bulletin Board • Individual Family Meetings • Parent Education Seminars • Early Intervention Groups • Substance Abuse Subtle Screening Inventory (SASSI)	• Targeted Individual Therapy • Targeted Group Therapy • Targeted Case Management • Assessment and Referral Assistance • Accountability Panels

(Kunert and Marnell 2002) Another Path is a supportive counseling program offered by The Foundation Schools to assist students to be alcohol and drug free.

What kind of joint is this anyway?

9

Creating & Maintaining
the Learning Community

Years ago the book *Lord of the Flies* (Golding 1959) painted a chilling picture of the society that would develop if a group of boys survived a plane crash on a remote island and had to deal with life without adult help. In his book *Code of the Street*, Elijah Anderson (1999) has described a real life counterpart in which there is "a competition in which 'winners' totally dominate 'losers,' and losing is a fate [that is] worse than death." This is a code of conduct in which might makes right, cooperation is for losers, and maintaining an image as an invincible winner seems crucial to survival. Needless to say, it is not a moral system compatible with the voluntary acceptance of a dependent learner's role. It is a worldview guaranteed to bypass academic endeavor.

    A learning community, on the other hand, is organized around the determination of a student majority to gain knowledge and skills. This requires a community where genuine accomplishments are respected and where student deficiencies give rise to mutual support and encouragement. The teacher is respected as a source of valuable information and help, not as an authority figure to be discredited and humiliated. It is not a perfect storybook world. Conflicts occur but they are resolved because the preeminence of the educational goal motivates everyone to direct most of his energies toward removing any obstacles to the process.

Creating the Learning Community

The first step in creating a learning community is to convince as many students as possible of the importance of education. It is usually possible to gain verbal acknowledgement of the value of education from almost any young person who agrees to attend school. Although this acknowledgement is abstract and often not discernable in the student's behavior, it does provide a basis for beginning to request school-ready and student-like actions from the youngsters. This approach, more fully discussed in chapter 1, allows the student to begin to define appropriate behavior as mature and goal directed rather than as a cowardly acceptance of external control. Therapists, teachers, and other staff should be poised to label positive behaviors as bravery, wisdom, and daring. In the milieu of the learning community, these actions are heroic. Admitting academic weaknesses or asking for help should be recognized as risk taking and a thrust into new territory. It is important that the staff sincerely views things in this way. What must be developed is not a manipulative, indirect means of gaining control, but a community in which adults and youngsters respect the perilous journey of learning and genuinely admire those who dare to pursue it. The advancing academic is not being good; she is waging a valiant war against ignorance. This brave soul deserves adult respect. The ethics of the school are derived from the school's responsibility to educate. Good behaviors are those that advance learning. Bad behaviors are those that interfere with the educational progress of the student or others in the school. These ethics are discussed frequently and connected with their solid source — the mutual commitment to learning.

It's important to recognize that some actions that advance learning do not fit the stereotypical view of the compliant, cooperative, respectful student. Students who take learning seriously may argue,

Creating and Maintaining the Learning Community

challenge the teacher, or get upset over the content of a class discussion. These behaviors have to be welcomed even when they need to be modulated because of group needs. After all, passion is evidence of serious commitment and genuine personal involvement in the classroom proceedings. We learn and retain when both our emotions and our thought processes are fully engaged. This is true in psychotherapy. It is also true in other educational settings.

Teaching students to respect each other's toil is more complicated. If adults can honestly portray the attitudes described above they will start the process. However, bullying, belittling, and intimidation are strongly ingrained in today's youth culture. Active efforts to control these behaviors are essential. These efforts begin with *all* staff confronting *all* bullying. These behaviors must be labeled as bullying even when students protest that they were only "playing" or "kidding around." When there is inequality between individuals the more vulnerable person does not experience in-your-face joking as amusing. This is a crucial point since peers with equal social standing frequently engage in hostile banter and playful conflict. Even this aggression may be excessive at times and lead to fights, but it is not perceived by the equal partner as harassment or intimidation.

Most students of school violence view bullying from a perspective of power dynamics (Twemlow, Fonagy, and Sacco 2001). The bully is deliberately trying to gain status at the expense of the weaker or less popular victim. These authors point out that bullying can be openly sadistic, verbally or physically, or it can be more subtle *social bullying* that takes the form of rumor mongering and ostracizing of chosen victims. These latter approaches are especially utilized by some social groups to exclude and torment other youngsters and promote an appearance of superiority.

Educational and therapeutic efforts should be focused on the three participants in the process: the bully, the victim, and the bystander. The last group is particularly important since most bullies require an appreciative audience. Those students who laugh when a victim is teased require evaluation. Sometimes they identify with the bully and are vicariously enjoying the victim's torment. Others are frightened and laugh to placate the bully so *they* can avoid being tormented. Each bystander should be carefully evaluated to discover what each one gains from their active or passive complicity in the bullying process.

The bullies need clear, honest, and calm confrontation that both labels their behavior as bullying and firmly forbids those actions. This limit setting is only the first step in the intervention. The bully's motivation and dynamics also need to be understood. According to Hare (1998) approximately one percent of them are youngsters whose lack of empathy, anxiety, or guilt over their sadistic actions meet criteria for true psychopathy. The vast majority of bullies are more complicated and fortunately more treatable. Many of these youngsters have themselves been bullied earlier, either in their families or in the community. Some are using the false sense of triumph that comes from easy conquests over the vulnerable to avoid facing more realistic challenges in their own lives. Still others cling to grandiosity as a substitute for a sense of personal competence and find the power surge of crushing others a necessary reassurance. There is simply no substitute for finding out the motives of each individual bully.

It can be difficult for the therapist to empathize with a student who is primarily interested in hurting other students mentally or physically. Nonetheless, if we do not extend ourselves to understand, we are at risk of being drawn into the vicious cycle of aggression, punishment, and teaching lessons — the very cycle we are trying to interrupt. We must try to understand why the bully wants and needs the sense of power achieved at the expense of humiliating and damaging another person. That knowledge will help us to find less damaging and even constructive alternatives to meet the same needs.

On the other hand, victims usually attract our sympathy. In fact, they do need staff protection, but they need more. Victims need many things. They can use advice about avoiding circumstances that increase the likelihood of being bullied, such as going into areas of the school where staff cannot supervise activities. Some-

Creating and Maintaining the Learning Community

times they need help with their social skills. Almost always they need the opportunity to deal with their feelings about being victimized and their anger that adults have not protected them. In all these interventions it is important to avoid blaming the victim for the event. Many youngsters who are targeted by bullies have physical or psychological characteristics that may not be attractive. Some of these may be partially or totally correctable with tactful direction of their therapist. Many victims have hidden problems that unconsciously lead them into situations and relationships where they are likely to be victimized. For example, some adolescent girls may be drawn to macho, bullying boys and end up in abusive relationships. If one assumes there is no voluntary action that does not produce a psychological gain –whether obvious or hidden- one will remember that all behavior is motivated. In exploring these issues it is important to retain sympathy for the victims and recognize that the actions that produce pain for them are usually driven by powerful, hidden forces in themselves of which they are only dimly aware.

> *Clarice's father deserted the family when Clarice was an infant. However, Clarice blamed her mother for her loss and idealized her father in spite of his total neglect of her and her siblings. At age fifteen she became involved with an unemployed, alcoholic twenty-seven-year-old man. When he drank he became verbally and physically abusive to Clarice. Later, motivated by guilt, he would buy her gifts. Clarice accepted these presents with tears of joy, always convinced that his contrition augured well for the future of the relationship. Her therapist, who had no idea of the man's age, questioned the source of her bruises on one occasion, suspecting abuse. Clarice became furious and accused the therapist of trying to ruin her happiness. It was months later before the girl could look honestly at the hidden origins of her choice of romantic partners.*

THE LEARNING ALLIANCE

Direct work with the bully begins with and depends upon the consistent and tireless confrontation of the behavior. Bullies almost never refer themselves for help in giving up the habit. They do not see themselves as bullies. Some youngsters are bullies in one situation and play different roles in other situations. It is up to the adults around them to define such behavior as a problem. Follow-up studies show that this is a correct definition. Bullies do tend to fare poorly in their future development. Psychotherapy for the bully includes empathy training, inquiry regarding earlier victimization in his or her life, and value restructuring. Often there is an opportunity for direct work with the bullying behavior since these youngsters are often intimidating in their interaction with the therapist. This provides chances to help the student to recognize the pattern and gradually understand its origins and finally to explore alternative and less destructive strategies for relating to others.

Maintaining the Learning Community
The learning community, like true love, does not run smoothly. Peer conflicts, conflicts between staff and students, conflicts between staff members, conflicts with parents and other community members, even dramatic events outside the school can all disrupt the learning community. These occurrences should not cause alarm but should be viewed as opportunities to teach and to reaffirm the value of the school culture. The essence of the learning community is in the process of its ongoing re-creation. The adaptive skills of verbalizing negative feelings, mediating conflict, crafting compromises, and reestablishing self-determined order are as much a part of the successful educational experience as mastering basic math.

The response to crisis is a crucial element in maintaining the learning community. Advance preparation and anticipation of likely crisis events help to protect the staff from the intense contagious effects that are created by major program disruptions. When clashes between students escalate to threatened or actual physical altercations, it is difficult for other students to stay calm. If the fight spreads it can run out of control, creating near riot conditions. In this and other situations

Creating and Maintaining the Learning Community

staff can remain calmer if they are clearly aware of their responsibilities and can actively help solve the problem. For example, students and staff should know in advance that uninvolved students should leave the area of conflict if fighting erupts. Staff should communicate clearly with one another. If two or three staff members are actively involved in separating the combatants, other staff can take responsibility for crowd control. Any student with strong connections with one of the fighters should receive special help in resisting the urge to jump into the conflict. The staff should be trained in techniques of therapeutic holding to ensure the safety of students and staff. Staff should have an understanding of the continuum of interventions so that most emergencies can be prevented and physical restraint is a rarely used last resort. However, in today's violent society, extreme outbursts, sometimes even requiring police intervention, do occur. Every school must have a well-considered safety plan for all possible contingencies and a trained crisis team to implement it.

Managing the aftermath of crisis situations is equally important. Staff and students need the opportunity to ventilate and process their feelings, which often include varying mixtures of anger, fear, and shame. The school leadership needs to listen even when staff members are overreacting and using inflammatory expressions — "it was a riot"; "it was totally out of control"; "I was really scared." These are common statements. They represent subjective but very real emotional reactions and should be accepted as such. However, it is important to review the events in detail since the actual risks are often much smaller than they seem in the heat of the uproar. For example, angry adolescents can sound extremely threatening while keeping their destructive impulses under control fairly well. They are talking destruction but their actions are not harmful. Immediately following an emotional conflagration, everyone — staff and student — who demonstrated self-control and limited permanent damage to the learning community should be strongly complimented. Those who lost control to some extent need to be calmly confronted and challenged to develop new adaptive strategies for handling their anger without damaging the learning process. Sadly, at times there will be some students who demonstrate truly dangerous behavior and little or no self-control; those students must be removed from the learning community through hospitalization, residential placement, or expulsion.

Another potential threat to the learning community is the influence of negative leaders. Some students are threatened by the values of the learning community. They fear that their prestige and status will diminish if the code of the street is replaced by respect for academic accomplishment. Their anxiety leads them to criticize, ridicule, and subvert the positive operation of the school. Their influence can be quite destructive, particularly in the early stages of community development.

It is important to meet their challenge head on. First, one should try to understand their behavior. Are they coming to school for some other purpose than to gain an education? Do they sincerely believe that learning can occur when the class or group therapy is being disrupted? Have they forgotten that the rules and structure exist merely to make the classroom or group therapy conducive to learning? If they are truly disinterested in gaining an education, have they discussed their contrary behaviors with their parent or guardian?

It is sometimes useful to acknowledge their power and skills. "I know you can make the class laugh whenever you want to." "I know some of the other students are afraid of you." "You're really good at pointing out the things that other people need to improve- you're a good observer." Such acknowledgements need to be quickly followed by a challenge to use those strengths to help the learning process rather than impeding it. It is important to avoid rejecting the negative leader. A sincere effort to draw him or her into the community should be extended and continued — even in the face of initial disinterest or outright disdain. Any positive response should be acknowledged with warmth but in a matter-of-fact manner — too much adult enthusiasm may be viewed as manipulation.

If the negative leader offers compromise, the offer should be carefully considered. If the student says, "I tell you what. I will stay in this classroom but I'm not going to do all that work. It's stupid." Then

Creating and Maintaining the Learning Community

the teacher might respond like this: "I'm glad you're willing to stay. Can we go over the work you don't want to do? I'm worried that I might leave some gaps in your education if we skip too much. Perhaps we can look at the possibility of doing some later or maybe you can work with your therapist around this. Unfortunately it is hard work to learn all you need to know."

Of course, this is not delivered all at once as a lecture. It is a mind-set and a general approach that must be tailored to individual styles. The therapist's role in these situations is to support the teacher and to help fellow staff deal with the angry feelings stirred by youngsters who interfere with the education of others.

Larger groups, such as community meetings, can be used to remind other students of the importance of learning and the behaviors that nurture the learning community. It is rarely helpful to identify the negative leader publicly or to overtly ask fellow students to control the miscreant's negative actions. It can be helpful to remind the student body that laughing at disruptive behavior or teasing may give the message that they want fellow students to act in those ways. The students can be challenged in this way: "I want each of you to ask yourself if your are helping to create a good atmosphere for learning." Public confrontations of the negative student by staff should be respectful. Disrespectful responses from students should not be allowed to pass without comment and intervention. The school should have a behavioral continuum of consequences that should be calmly applied to assist the offending student to regain control and demonstrate school-ready behavior.

Over the long haul, positive reenforcement of school-ready and student-like behavior shape the learning community even more than curtailing crises and effectively managing negative leaders. Genuine respect for students who make a serious commitment to scholarly work and to helping their classmates learn will gradually alter the attitudes and actions of most students. This is not to say that a functioning learning community is all work and no play. Children of all ages have an intense need to play and socialize — so do the adults who work with them. In a healthy learning community, students and

THE LEARNING ALLIANCE

staff are willing to interrupt play in order to get down to work and are willing to delay playing until the necessary job is done. After work is completed celebration is in order. As a rule it is better for the rewards to be rewards and not bribes or conditions for working.

There are two types of rewards: wages, if you will, designated in advance to be expected after assigned work is completed; and symbols of mutual achievement distributed during celebrations of group accomplishments, which should usually arrive as unexpected gifts. For example, if a student meets all criteria for advancement in a behavior-modification program, he receives the privileges and prizes appropriate to that level of achievement – a wage in a sense. On the other hand, if an English class cooperates and works so that everyone moves up a letter grade, the teacher might surprise the group with a congratulatory pizza party – a symbol of mutual achievement.

Staff should always remember that the learning process itself and the membership in the learning community are the most valuable gifts and prizes that we have to offer. More important than any material exchange is the emotional interchange among students, teachers, and other important staff — especially the program assistants, crisis therapists, and other mentors who have extensive, close interactions with the students. The age of the student is important in determining appropriate reenforcement. The elementary student, especially in the beginning grades, responds comfortably to adult praise. "You have been so good today." "I'm so proud of you!" "Your work is beautiful. Let me give you a hug." Since the younger child works primarily to gain adult approval, such comments strongly support academic effort. Similar comments to high school students would be experienced as infantalizing, demeaning and controlling.

Adolescents, even middle school adolescents, need to feel included in decisions and need to enter voluntarily into the learning alliance. Their decision to enter this pact is smart, mature, admirable, logical, and very sane. It is not obedient, compliant, sweet, nice, or a personal gift to the teacher or therapist. It is crucial to keep this in mind when recognizing their work. They are equals whose contributions to the learning process are essential. Their efforts should be

Creating and Maintaining the Learning Community

respectfully acknowledged. "I really respect the effort you have put into this assignment." "I must say I admire someone who can get down to work when she has a lot of things on her mind." "I can tell you are taking this subject matter quite seriously." Therapists can also inquire, "Are you feeling good about your work?" If the student is ambivalent about his success or misinterprets the nature of the task, the therapist should patiently explore this material. For example, if the student complains, "I'm tired of kissing that teacher's ass," the therapist can explore the youngster's feeling that he is only working to gain approval or avoid punishment rather than excelling for his personal benefit. Reviewing personal goals and motivations for academic achievement can help the student reconfirm voluntary membership in the learning community. If students say they are tired or that the effort required is too great, they should receive sympathy, support, and encouragement. Sometimes it helps to identify with the student and agree that most worthwhile things seem to require an inordinate amount of work. One might even add, "Man, I wish I could just wave a wand and grant you a good education. Unfortunately, I don't know any way to get there except the way you're struggling." The therapist's job is to help the student maintain focus on the main goal, while also helping the student deal with the many distracting events and feelings that inevitably occur on the journey.

THE LEARNING ALLIANCE

Extra Credit 22

Two Forms of Bullying: Aggressive and Passive

Characteristics of the Aggressive Bully
- Initiates aggression toward peers
- Fearless, coercive, tough, and impulsive
- Inclination toward violence, desire to dominate others, and expresses little sympathy toward his/her victims
- Commits open attacks on his/her victims
- Enjoys being in control and wishes to subdue others
- Cognitively distorts the meaning of his/her victim's behavior
- Overreacts in ambiguous situations
- Views the world with a paranoid's eyes

Characteristics of the Passive Bully
- Appears to be dependent, insecure, and anxious
- Participates in bullying but usually doesn't initiate aggression
- Isolates and excludes others from the group
- If s/he sees aggressive bully being rewarded, likely to follow suit
- Lacks defined social status in peer group
- Affiliates with aggressive bully

(Adapted from Newman, Horne, and Bartolomucci 2000; Olweus 1994; Ross 1996)

Creating and Maintaining the Learning Community

Extra Credit 23

Prevention, Intervention and Bullying

Preventing Bullying and Victimization
- Establish zero tolerance policy of no bullying
- Reinforce helping, non-aggressive and on-task behaviors
- Teach social skills
- Teach problem-solving and decision-making skills
- Help students become aware of their strengths
- Model respect for others
- Maintain a positive attitude
- Use praise to reinforce good behaviors

Interventions for Bullies
- Help them understand victim's point of view
- Teach them to list behaviors that need to be changed
- Use written contracts
- Teach nonaggressive and nonbullying alternative behaviors
- Use role reversals and role plays to help bullies understand what it feels like to be the victim
- Immediately defuse bullying and address the issue with the bully privately later
- Teach anger management
- Record bullying incidents and interventions used

Interventions for Victims
- Teach them social and coping skills to help them deal with conflicts
- Provide support by creating an "open door" policy

continued on the folowing page...

THE LEARNING ALLIANCE

...continued on the folowing page
- Teach confidence and self-esteem building skills
- Assist in identifying coping skills they may want to learn
- Use written contracts
- Teach verbal assertiveness skills
- Teach physical assertiveness skills using posture and eye contact

Preventing Bullying and Victimization
- Establish and implement a peer mediation program
- Conduct open discussions about bullying and victimization
- Teach how to recognize and identify characteristics and behaviors of bullies
- Teach the lasting effects of bullying and victimization
- Teach collaborative conflict resolution skills

(Fried and Fried 1996; Hazler 1996; Kraiser 1996; Newman, Horne, and Bartolomucci 2000)

Creating and Maintaining the Learning Community

Extra Credit 24

Four Cornerstones of the Learning Community

Respect for children and adolescents we have chosen to serve

1. Respect is often confused with obedience. Discipline for obedience may be an initial goal for students who lack self-control but without discipline for responsibility, we will never produce genuinely respectful youth. Adults should not exercise control over students but adults should help students to practice and develop self-control — control over themselves. Also we must not forget that respect is a reciprocal process and adults will never gain the respect of youth they dislike. Only by giving students respect and responsibility will they give it back to adults in genuine ways.

Purpose and timing of interventions for individual students

2. Based on the way we present "the moment" to a student, it is not an opportunity for us as adults to express ourselves, to address our personal likes and dislikes. Rather, we give students the gift of opportunity to correct, to practice what has been difficult to do — to make a good decision, to change. As adults, we need to step back from a situation, even as it's happening, and focus on the student's feelings rather than our own. We need to be fully conscious of the purpose of that particular intervention with that particular student and at that particular time.

continued on the folowing page...

THE LEARNING ALLIANCE

...continued on the folowing page
We must be able to professionally justify that that indeed was the teachable moment and the appropriate corrective and therapeutic response. Every bit as much as the student is not in control, that is the degree to which we must be.

A belief that we can and we will make a difference

3. The histories of our students are difficult to read. They are often lives filled with abuse, neglect, despair, and failure after failure. And when our students come to us and replicate the fear, abuse, and terror they have experienced, it is easy to lose hope. Listen to the voices of our children and adolescents. If they have experienced such trauma in their lives and they have not lost hope, then why should we? Hear them tell us. Focus on strengths; focus on building trust; target competence. Reach out to students in good faith. Move from hopelessness to hope and helpfulness.

To be consistent and to remain consistent

4. None of the previous points will matter much or take hold if we apply these cornerstones on one day but not the next. Our students may have a lot of inconsistencies in their lives; they don't need more of that from us. Every day, come to work with unconditional acceptance of our students who themselves come back day after day for more of what we offer them. If you know what students have missed and you believe they have missed it – the nurturing and the meeting of their most basic needs, then you will want to be consistent. In being consistent, you will make every effort to help

Creating and Maintaining the Learning Community

our students become more whole and begin to function in healthier ways.

(based on "The Foundation Schools' Four Cornerstones" by Denese Lombardi, Director of The Foundation School of Alexandria)

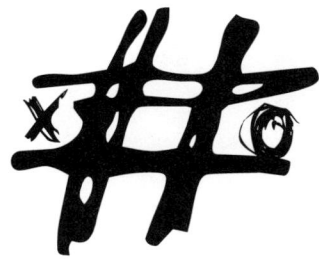

I can
only talk
to Mr.
Jones.

10

The Paraprofessional
Their Role in School Psychotherapy

Most special education school staffs are multidisciplinary. Physicians, teachers, social workers, counselors, psychologists, art therapists, music therapists, librarians, speech and language pathologists, and others must learn to work together and to appreciate the special skills each can bring to the educational effort. This task requires a great deal of effort and goodwill. But the effort to maximize the contribution of paraprofessional workers may be even more daunting. Almost all schools have teacher aides, crisis counselors, program assistants, one-on-ones, mentors, or other individuals who are actively involved in the students' care but who usually have not completed a professional degree. This chapter refers to these staff members as paraprofessionals or program assistants interchangeably, recognizing that their roles and titles vary from one program to another.

Regardless of what they are called, they often have more direct interaction with students than do the members of the professional staff. In most programs these are the staff members who deal with emergency situations, encountering the students at the height of emotional vulnerability and availability. Because of frequent, informal, and

THE LEARNING ALLIANCE

emotionally rich contact, students often become very attached to these staff members. When the student encounters other staff members there is usually a clear objective of the interaction. Teachers are usually teaching; therapists are usually treating. Although program assistants do both at times, they also have more opportunity to chat informally and somewhat socially with students.

They Know their Students Well

The program assistants know the students well as individuals. When they also have extensive experience and seniority, they often are more comfortable with the school program and the needs of the students than are young professionals or professionals who are new to the specific school. These facts provide many opportunities for misunderstandings and hidden conflict. Insecure professionals may find it difficult to accept guidance from the paraprofessional and the paraprofessional may interpret the inexperienced professional's early awkwardness and uncertainty as incompetence.

In fact, both groups need each other. The professional can benefit greatly from insights arising from the students' more relaxed and sometimes more open communication with program assistants. Often students reveal feelings or information to the trusted paraprofessional in hopes that other staff will be informed. It is common for paraprofessionals to be the first to hear that a child is suicidal or homicidal. Perhaps it is less threatening for many students to expose uncomfortable feelings to someone who seems like an older friend rather than some less approachable person with a degree and title. These confidences must be shared with the responsible professional staff member — but without causing the student to feel betrayed. This can be done if the paraprofessional has genuine respect for the therapist or teacher who needs the information. When this is true the student is accepting — and perhaps even relieved — that appropriate help is being mobilized.

How is it possible to develop this degree of trust and respect between professionals and paraprofessional staff? It begins with showing respect to the paraprofessional staff. Since these staff members

The Paraprofessional's Role

often perceive themselves as having low status in the school hierarchy, it is incumbent on the remainder of the staff, beginning with the school director, to verbalize and demonstrate their recognition of the important role of the paraprofessional. This appreciation must go beyond recognizing the paraprofessional's vital role in maintaining order. If support staff view themselves as babysitters, cops, bouncers, or enforcers they are unlikely to function as thoughtful, contributing members of the treatment team.

This does not mean that all input from paraprofessionals is blindly accepted. Support staff, particularly those who have had little experience in a treatment setting, may believe that defensive statements from students represent facts. For example, angry or frustrated students often say they don't care about the opinions of others or may say they are only in school because of some manipulative goal. This fact led one honest but inexperienced paraprofessional to say, "I'm still trying to figure out if these kids have problems or if they're just bad." He was congratulated for raising the question since it gave the opportunity to explain how troubled youngsters — especially adolescents — may prefer to be seen as courageously evil rather then ill or disturbed. After a few years of experience, however, it is the paraprofessionals who are teaching these truths to new professional staff when they are overwhelmed by the tough and aggressive presentation of our students. As one experienced paraprofessional said, "If a kid says he doesn't care, he's just saying he hasn't yet figured out how to succeed." That kind of insight is priceless.

All staff members require orientation and ongoing reminders of the importance of image and peer acceptance in the life of adolescents. Recognizing the need to appear independent of adult authority and contemptuous of adult values helps staff members understand some of the inappropriate statements and behavior students demonstrate when they are in the company of peers. This representation often differs considerably from the concerns and attitudes they may reveal when alone with an adult. Anderson's *Code of the Street* (1999) describes the self-protective necessity of combative posturing by some youngsters who actually have very conventional goals. In the case of students with emotional problems, what you see is by no means always what you get.

Experienced program assistants are well aware of these affectations and often have profound insights into the motivations, social problems, and current status of students. In time they even learn to translate these insights into proper professional jargon, but the wise professional listens to the substance rather than the form even before this happens. Many schools have found that it is helpful to cut across professional language boundaries by training all staff in a single theoretical approach suitable to a range of backgrounds. One useful model is *Life Space Crisis Intervention (LSCI)* as detailed by Long, Wood, and Fecser (2001). The system provides a common language and easily grasped categories of behavior that allow all staff to communicate more clearly. LSCI is an effective strategy by which paraprofessionals and professionals can use classroom conflict as an opportunity to refocus students to new insight about their behavior. LSCI empowers staff to covert the classroom conflict into a meaningful learning experience for students by helping them discover the motivating forces behind their behavior and define clear goals to change their behavior in future incidents. Other useful models include Eggert's (1994) *Anger Management for Youth* and *Aggression Replacement Therapy (ART)* as described by Goldstein (1987).

When paraprofessionals sense that they have been accepted into the inner circle of professionalism and are full-fledged members of a cohesive team, they are freed to appreciate the contributions of the other specialists. This respect leads them to want each student to have full advantage of the expertise available in the program. They are likely to convey a sense of positive collaboration. "Let's take this to Ms. Smith, she's the person who can really help us with this one."

Therapeutic Holds

Because of their less defined role and their intimate contact with students, paraprofessionals are at special risk for many boundary problems. They are the staff members who are most often involved in the *therapeutic hold* of students. We define *therapeutic hold* as the behavior

The Paraprofessional's Role

management techniques used by one or more trained staff that involves safe and nonabusive bodily contact with a student. Therapeutic holds are applied when clinical judgment indicates that the student is: at risk of hurting herself or himself or others; or making efforts to cause significant damage to school property. Therapeutic holds should not be used as a first behavioral intervention. They should be used as a final resort. Therapeutic holds should only be used after documented failure of less restrictive interventions. Therapeutic holds are designed to help students regain control of their own behavior. The intense feelings of fear, anger, and counter-aggression stirred by the process of struggling with an out-of-control student can lead to use of excessive force. Detailed, repeated, and ongoing training regarding the indications for the use of therapeutic holds as well as the proper techniques to avoid injury both to the student and staff member is crucial.

There are several well-designed, proven approaches used for training of staff. *Therapeutic Aggression Control Techniques (TACT-2)* (Parese 1997) and *Non-Abusive Psychological and Physical Intervention (NAPPI)* (Lalemand 2002) are two of the best approaches used in residential as well as day programs for students with emotional disturbance. All staff involved in therapeutic holds need the opportunity to discuss their feelings and receive supportive supervision. Students who have been involved in therapeutic holds need the opportunity to process the event, express any angry feelings, and accept their responsibility in precipitating the crisis. The experience should be used as a teaching opportunity that the student can utilize to learn new and more adaptive ways to respond to upsets. Often it is wise to have mediation between the student and the staff members directly involved in the therapeutic hold. This opportunity allows the student to understand that the hold was designed to protect the student from doing something he or she would later regret and was not an act of aggression.

It is also wise to look carefully at the reasons why a student ends up in a therapeutic hold. Therapists need to be alert to the dynamics that lead some students to repeated holds. Some male adolescents

THE LEARNING ALLIANCE

(and even younger students) provoke physical restraint as part of image posturing. They want to impress peers with their fearless challenge to male staff and the battle they put up in resisting the physical restraint. Other students, male and female, may incite a therapeutic hold to gratify sexually oriented wishes for body contact. Usually they are totally unaware of the pathological needs that drive their behavior. Fortunately, most students who require the use of a therapeutic hold are merely testing the safety of the environment. They often fear their own anger and their omnipotent destructive fantasies. They are calmed and comforted when they realize that the school staff can control them. Unlike the pathological needs for therapeutic holds, this need is almost developmental since many of these youngsters have never experienced competent, strong, consistent, and kind limit-setting behavior. They respond with psychological growth and do not require repeated therapeutic holds.

The Paraprofessional Acting as Parent

The temptation to paraprofessionals to be drawn into a parenting role with students may be quite seductive. Students, especially those without available parents, tend to look to front line staff as substitute parents. To some extent this is healthy and constructive. Encouragement, appreciation, and advice and counsel coming from respected mentors whose guidance is accepted is a major factor in many students' progress. The students often say, "Ms. Jones is like a second mother to me." It is important, however, not to cross the line and begin to take on actual parental responsibilities. Staff should not provide money, give individual gifts, drive the student on errands, or engage in other activities that would blur the distinction between professional behavior and parenting. If the students require help of this kind, the school should provide it — not individual staff members. The reasons are compelling. Staff members cannot make the full commitment required by parenthood. Staff members, as well as students, may move to new responsibilities, disrupting the continuity necessary to parenthood. If all good things come from an individual staff member, the separation can be

The Paraprofessional's Role

devastating. On the other hand, if the staff member has used the bond with the student to strengthen the youngster's connection to the entire program then the child is not abandoned. Of course, this approach requires the school to formalize simple procedures through which staff can arrange for any needed assistance for the students. In the case of older students, it is often wise to provide a context in which the student can work for their grant to avoid excessive dependency or a sense of shame about accepting charity.

Boundary Issues Again

All school staff members are at risk of being accused of, or of being actually involved in romantic or sexual entanglements with students in their care. Paraprofessionals, because of the more unstructured nature of their interaction with students, may be especially vulnerable. The most visible example of this problem involves young male paraprofessionals who are frequently the object of female students' passionate crushes. Similar infatuations occur between male students and women paraprofessionals, teachers, and therapists. Therapists are perhaps better prepared to recognize and understand the intensity and the real basis of these transference feelings. However, these crushes can create serious problems for all concerned. Some students make very active efforts to seduce staff members. The staff members are fond of the students and, perhaps at some level, flattered by the student's obvious admiration. When feelings get a bit intense most staff members recognize their danger and ask for help. But there are occasions, especially if the student has convinced the adult that no one else understands or is trying to help, when liaisons do occur. This is usually a gradual process, often apparent to coworkers, which can be interrupted before major damage to the student and to the career of the staff person occurs. The school must take public and immediate administrative action to halt such behavior — even if it means terminating the employment of an otherwise competent and effective staff member. If the offending staff member is a professional, the appropriate disciplinary committee should be notified. In all cases, the caretakers of the child must be fully informed and the school should give complete cooperation in any resulting legal actions. Occasionally, other staff members may defend the offender, citing the active seductiveness of the student, his or her age, and other presumably mitigating circumstances. In fact none of these justify the betrayal of trust involved in this action.

A more common occurrence is the unfounded accusation of inappropriate sexual behavior. This accusation can come from a student who is angry with a staff member and wishes to create problems or even have the staff member fired. Sometimes the accusation comes from a student who alleges that the staff member is involved with someone else in the school. In this case the vindictiveness may be directed toward the staff member or the named student. The accuser may want the other student to be embarrassed or embroiled in controversy. In other cases, the accusation may be anonymous and the motive completely obscure. In any case the staff member needs to see that the school administration does not assume guilt and is willing to carefully explore the facts of the situation. Usually when one explores the concrete details of where and when the alleged events occurred, who was present, and other facts, the falseness of the claim becomes apparent. After the fact-finding, the accuser's behavior can be addressed within the usual school rules and consequences as well as approached therapeutically.

None of these potential problems should overshadow the tremendous value of paraprofessionals in the school setting. Students, therapists, and teachers need the insight and skills of this group. There is no substitute for the wealth of information and observation they bring to the understanding of each student. The relaxed, somewhat unhurried, informal relationship they have with students opens doors that may be closed to the narrowly defined role of the professional. If they are included as full partners in the educational effort they can interpret and implement very complex and subtle remediation efforts.

The paraprofessional, like all other members of the school staff, is effective when he or she is an integrated member of a structured continuum of helpers. All members of this group have the responsibility

The Paraprofessional's Role

to provide one another with recognition of valuable interventions, validation of the value of all, and comfortable confrontation when someone is having difficulty performing at the level required by the school's mission and the students' needs. The learning alliance requires us to expect full responsibility from all participants.

Other School Support Staff

The *school administrative assistant or school secretary* sometimes is the safe person that doesn't take away points for misbehaviors but can lead the student back to the therapist. Darnita was referred to our schools because of failure and rejection in several public schools. The few times she attended public schools, if she had a problem in any of her classes, teachers had the terrible habit of sending her to the principal's office. After one too many visits, the school secretary put her to work. Darnita excelled at several tasks assigned to her. Do you know who acted up in order to be sent to the office so she could feel needed and wanted? Why couldn't the school administrator and the teachers collaborate with the school secretary and Darnita to balance the need for her education and her need to belong and help out in the office?

The *speech and language pathologist (SLP)* can open the window to communication and understanding for the student. At the same time the SLP can work with the psychotherapist regarding the student's limited expression, auditory processing problems, and so forth. The speech and language pathologist can help the psychotherapist understand the speech and language disability and help the student deal with some of the expressive and receptive issues of language in private psychotherapy.

> *Lakeisha, a fourteen-year-old nominal seventh grader, was referred to The Foundation Schools because of truancy, failing grades, explosive outbursts, multiple runaways, and, finally, expulsion from public school because of fighting. Shortly after being expelled she was admitted to a psychiatric hospital because of marijuana abuse, depression, chronic*

anger, threatening behavior at home, refusal to communicate with her mother, and suicidal threats. She was prescribed Paxil and Trilafon which she did not take on discharge.

Lakeisha, in spite of all her problems, was pleased to be accepted into school. She was withdrawn and suspicious but willing to cooperate. The admission evaluation revealed a Receptive Language Score of 69 on the Clinical Evaluation of Language Function which placed her in the second percentile. Her Expressive Language Score was in the thirty-ninth percentile. On the Woodcock-Johnson Psycho-Educational Battery her Letter-Word Identification level was first grade, eighth month. Her Broad Reading Score on the same test was 2.2.

Lakeisha's speech and language evaluation revealed a moderate impairment due to a very limited vocabulary, impaired speech intelligibility, and marked impairment of written language.

Lakeisha had complicating family issues as well. She was very fond of her mother who was a loving parent. However, the mother suffered from a chronic, recurrent illness, which periodically rendered her unavailable to Lakeisha and even, at times, resulted in emergency hospitalization. In an effort to protect Lakeisha, the mother said very little about her illness and did not warn Lakeisha when she was relapsing. The result, in fact, was to keep Lakeisha in constant fear that her mother might get worse and might die without warning. Lakeisha was also frightened that she might inherit her mother's illness.

Not that Lakeisha was revealing any of those personal concerns when she entered Foundation School. She was distant, frequently asked to be left alone, and did little school work. When she was referred for weekly speech and language treatment she balked. She claimed she had no problems. With much encouragement from her classroom teacher and her therapist, accompanied by frequent gentle

The Paraprofessional's Role

confrontation about her sometimes unintelligible speech, Lakeisha began to attend. Gradually she began to see the benefits of speech therapy and, after a time, was requesting the assistance of her speech therapist with school assignments. At this point, and for the first year, the primary emphasis of speech therapy was to improve her receptive vocabulary, a daunting task in view of her limited ability to understand definitions and her difficulties in making word associations. Lakeisha came to understand that her difficulties in understanding classroom instruction and even answering simple questions were due to her language deficits.

Her therapist emphasized Lakeisha's strengths such as her leadership abilities with peers, common sense, and her compassionate and warm nature. The first goal was to link her school success with regular attendance. This required work with Lakeisha's mother. She was helped to understand that daily attendance was essential for students such as Lakeisha who need extra help in order to catch up. The mother's dependence on Lakeisha, especially during episodes of illness, were explored and the mother was connected with community resources that could help her in times of need.

Her therapist also focused on Lakeisha's explosive and violent reaction to frustration and conflict. Lakeisha was helped to identify her feelings and was introduced to new behavioral and coping strategies. These were practiced through role playing. As Lakeisha's ability to express herself and her understanding of her learning disability and her emotional response to it grew, the therapy widened. Lakeisha's self-esteem and her attitudes toward her sexuality became prominent themes.

After this period of preparatory work, Lakeisha was ready, in fact eager, to learn to read. She was basically starting from scratch. Her English teacher worked with her individually, patiently teaching her how to decode words she did not know and slowly growing her recognition of sight words. The teacher taught her to look for key words in sentences to help her guess "mystery words" and increase her comprehension. At the end of that school year, Lakeisha proudly told everyone, "Mrs. H. taught me to read." Lakeisha was also enrolled in a reading remediation group which uses an organized approach to improving reading skills. The collaborative effort helped Lakeisha to gain self-control and self-esteem. She became a popular, positive leader in the school and a successful student.

Bus drivers and bus aides sometimes spend up to three hours a day with students; these people also need to work with therapists and school personnel. A psychotic boy at one of our schools found one of the bus aides particularly calming and sought her out almost daily to chat briefly.

Sometimes the *janitor/maintenance personnel* might connect the student with the therapist or visa versa because of vocational interests. Lloyd always wanted to be a janitor as long as his mom could remember. Lloyd wanted to quit school until he had several serious talks with the school janitor. The janitor not only had finished high school but he had gone to college for two years. Lloyd finally finished school and now works as janitor at a residential school.

Volunteers in some schools work well with therapists, teachers, and other faculty. Volunteers may also help with follow-up studies or other research. *Outside agencies* (Department of Social Services (DSS), mentors, support programs, tutors, community resources) should have a connection with the therapist who often helps to coordinate their efforts on behalf of students or families.

How can I help from way out here?

11

The Office Therapist
and School Problems

Although a therapeutic alliance is necessary in working on academic problems in any setting, for the office practitioner, it is crucial. The student patient and the patient's parents are usually the primary source of information about school. Even the parents' input will be compromised if the young patient views their involvement as nagging interference. Gaining the young person's active participation in addressing educational difficulties begins with a careful evaluation of the problem. A typical initial presentation includes worried parents with a child who may be minimizing the seriousness of the situation. This is understandable, since adults usually have a clearer understanding of the importance of education and since students may try to protect themselves from anxiety and shame through avoidance and denial. Thus, the child may see the educational concerns of the parents as their problem, not his or hers. Sometimes they are correct.

> Rodney was brought to therapy because his grades were Cs and Ds. The thirteen-year-old adopted boy attended one of

THE LEARNING ALLIANCE

the most competitive middle schools in the community. The parents were highly successful professionals. Rodney was a large, handsome, and pleasant youngster. He assured the therapist that he was doing his best in school. He was worried about his parents being upset with his grades but was unsure of what he could do to improve. He was hopeful that the therapist could help him. The parents did not want the therapist to contact Rodney's school. The therapist accepted this limitation temporarily but insisted on a thorough educational evaluation. The testing revealed that Rodney had an I.Q. of 73. Later, when the parents allowed the therapist to communicate with Rodney's school, he learned that this was a well-known fact that Rodney's parents refused to accept. Rodney and his family definitely needed therapy but not for Rodney's scholastic situation. He was, in fact, an overachiever.

This is not the typical situation. More often, the parents are correct in their concern and the student's school agrees that the child is underachieving. When that is true, the therapist is faced with the task of developing a learning alliance with the young student. Fortunately, most youngsters who are suitable for outpatient psychotherapy have considerable ego strength. As a rule, they are less defeated and dispirited than those youngsters whose problems have been so severe and chronic as to cause referral to special education settings. The defenses described earlier as characteristic of students in special education settings, are often there in these students as well, but not so ingrained and ossified. They are usually more easily available to the therapeutic process.

Once again, the first step is to build *Aspiration* for academic success. The techniques are the same as those described earlier. First, one explores the youngster's understanding of the role of learning in his hopes and plans. Factual information and relaxed discussion of future options can be very helpful in raising the student's opinion regarding the value of a broad and deep education. Once the

The Office Therapist and School Problems

student has formed a beginning therapeutic alliance with the therapist, a learning alliance can be developed — if the therapist consistently returns to educational issues as one important element of the therapy.

Exploring past educational experiences and traumatic events outside of school is an essential element of creating genuine aspiration. One needs to identify not only the events that soured the student on school, but the interpretations and mental elaboration the student may have added. Kennedy and Morton (1999) have called the former *key events* and the latter *visual overlay* and suggest that the combination often leads to an *outcome* that is detrimental to the youngster's educational efforts. See chapter 3 for a suggested format to help therapists understand the sources of negative attitudes toward school.

The process of helping the student develop *Inspiration* is somewhat more difficult for the outpatient therapist because less information regarding the student's skill level is available. Without direct and continuing communication with the student's teachers, it can be difficult to identify the youngster's strengths and track academic progress. However, much can be learned through having the youngster bring schoolwork to sessions, including both homework and graded papers. Therapist involvement with these materials provides an opportunity for modeling an enthusiastic and hopeful attitude toward the learning process and a chance to observe and cheer any progress the student is making. Direct observation of the student also can allow the therapist to detect attention problems and even specific learning problems. Over time, it can be possible to sort out which aspects of the school difficulty may be primary and which elements represent secondary defensive efforts to avoid psychological pain. The goal is to make an accurate diagnosis of the source or sources of the learning block and then to plan appropriate interventions.

In some cases this may involve tutoring, remediation, or even a transfer to a more appropriate school. In most cases, however, it is possible to develop the needed team through available sources in the youngster's school and in the community. For example, most colleges can provide names of students who are interested in serving as tutors at a reasonable cost. Many of these bright young people can even implement some remedial interventions, if these have been developed from an educational evaluation. The parents, the tutor, and the student will need a few meetings with the educational evaluator to make the test findings really useful in solving the problems (Cohen 1997). Cohen also suggests that a letter, containing a brief summary of the findings, written at the appropriate psychological and developmental level, should be mailed to the student. He has found that youngsters review such letters carefully, both alone and with adults, and that they add materially to the student's cooperation in the treatment process.

Collaboration with parents in treating school difficulties is crucial, yet it can be quite tricky. First, it is vitally important that the youngster firmly believes that the therapist is totally committed to the overall well-being of the student. Although it may be clear to the therapist that improving school performance is most definitely in the youngster's best interest, the student may initially see improving academics as entirely the agenda of parents, teachers, and other adults. Excessive involvement and identification with parental goals may lead your young client to feel that you are simply an undercover agent for all those nagging grownups. After the therapist has made significant progress on *Aspiration* and *Inspiration*, the parents can be more actively involved as allies in achieving what are now the student's goals. The parents will be more effective if the therapist can help them to take a constructive role. Many parents are exquisitely aware of the importance of education in our modern society. When their child is doing poorly in school, they are understandably distressed and frightened. Unfortunately, frightened people are not always able to use their best judgment and their creativity may be disrupted. Often the parents of troubled students need support and direction to maximize their effectiveness with their child. Too often, homework and school performance have become battlegrounds marked by angry entrenchment on both sides as the parents resort to threats and punishments and children be-

The Office Therapist and School Problems

come sullen, evasive, and resentful. The parents, as well as the student, need help in redefining the purpose of education and recognizing the necessity for wholehearted commitment on the part of the youngster.

Many parents have been convinced by their child's defensive posture that the youngster really does not care about school. The therapist can use his or her understanding of the truth of the situation to help the parents understand why and how the problem began and how it is sustained. Very few children and adolescents simply get up one morning and decide to fail. They always have reasons, which to them seem compelling and correct (Kennedy and Morton 1999). They cannot reverse this mindset without help. They cannot do better in school to please their parents, to escape punishment, or even to get everybody off their case. However, the troubled student needs help from parents — at whatever level the parent can provide. Even nonproductive involvement is recognized as caring even though the student cannot admit it during the highly stressful times.

When parents are led to offer constructive help and the youngster is prepared to work with them, a great deal can be accomplished. Most parents underestimate the power of their influence — even on adolescent children. If the parent is genuinely interested in academic matters, shares the student's triumphs, and takes a supportive role regarding problems, the youngster benefits greatly. Some of the helpful attitudes and approaches are detailed in chapter 6. In many cases, the parents of outpatients are more available and cooperative than the parents who have lived through the repeated failures and disappointments that lead to the placement of their children in special education settings. Several recent books aim to help parents and communities improve their children's school experience. All of them contain useful information and worthwhile suggestions. They are worth recommending to interested parents, but no book can substitute for the skilled clinician who is working to create a genuine atmosphere of cooperative effort – a learning alliance of student, parents, and school staff. See page 169 for a list of helpful books.

THE LEARNING ALLIANCE

The effort to collaborate with the student's school also begins with the parents. Some parents are hesitant to permit the therapist to contact the school Some of them are worried that they may stigmatize their child or at least draw negative attention by allowing a mental health practitioner to reveal that the child is in treatment. Others worry that the school may take less responsibility for the educational advancement of the child or lower their academic expectations if they view the child as troubled. In fact, school personnel are almost always aware that the child is conflicted and are often relieved to hear that the parents have sought help. Nonetheless, the therapist has to take such concerns seriously and patiently explore them while helping the parent understand the need for cooperation in resolving the problem. Parents also need to understand that some school personnel may be fooled by the student's bravado into believing that the youngster is cheerfully dismissing the whole issue. This is especially likely with adolescent boys, but can occur with other students as well. When they learn that the student is actually accepting help to improve the situation it can create a more accepting atmosphere for the student.

> *Michael, a thirteen-year-old eighth grader, was referred for therapy because of truancy and academic failure. He was depressed, actually in near-suicidal despair, but at school he maintained a happy-go-lucky façade. Since he was athletic and popular he didn't want to spoil his image. His mother bought his uncaring presentation until he insisted that he did not mind losing his athletic eligibility. Fortunately, she knew him well enough to recognize that he could never honestly say that. When the therapist contacted the school counselor she was delighted to have an ally in her effort to convince the teachers that Michael was disturbed, not just a wise guy and a goof-off.*

Once the parents are comfortable with school contact, the idea must be presented to the student. Surprisingly, many students have

The Office Therapist and School Problems

no objection, particularly once a trusting therapeutic alliance is in place. Some students offer suggestions about which school person should be called, naturally preferring those who seem more understanding toward them. It is wise to start with this person, using him to expand one's contacts since the student is likely to trust the steps suggested by his or her ally at school. The student is often more comfortable with therapist involvement in the school place than with direct parental contact. Having one's parents too visibly involved can lead to anticipated or real loss of status with peers.

The therapist should move slowly and carefully in early school contacts. Initially one should emphasize the very real need for information rather than one's own potential contribution to educational planning. Humility is necessary in this situation. The therapist's ideas about the student are based on one or two office visits per week, while school personnel have observed the youngster in a variety of settings and interactions for several hours each day. While the therapist may have better access to the student's motivations due to the intimacy and the confidentiality of therapy sessions, the school provides an invaluable source of behavioral data. One is well advised to do a great deal of listening and inquiring before hazarding any opinions. It is also wise to avoid being drawn into staff disagreements through siding with the staff person whose opinion is most favorable to the student or in closest agreement with one's own ideas. It is also wise to be very cautious in any discussion of the student's parents. Any negative comments, even given in jest, can come back to haunt the therapy. Maintaining this role requires some diplomacy and considerable empathy to understand the viewpoints of all the people important to the student's success. When one encounters anger or outrage directed at the student or parent it can be tempting to try to explain why the person acts as they do. Usually this is counterproductive and only leads the angry person to feel that you are condoning the misbehavior that has annoyed the school staff. It is usually more helpful to thank the person for the information and to indicate a willingness to address the problem in therapy. Later it may be possible to help the person develop

THE LEARNING ALLIANCE

a more positive view of your patient by mentioning some of the parent or child's strong points and asking if those are ever visible in school. Eventually it may be possible to gently re-frame the student's misbehavior. For example, one might say, "Yes, I've seen that sarcastic side of Charles myself. In our work it tends to show up when he's unsure of himself. I guess he more or less goes on the offensive to protect himself. It's too bad because it really puts people off."

If the school really welcomes a collaboration, it may be possible to widen the understanding of the student in many members of the school staff. However, it is important to remember that the primary mission of the public school is to educate all the young people entrusted to their care. The psychological needs of one student, no matter how legitimate, will never be allowed to disrupt the educational progress of the student group. Your therapy with the student and his or her family must accept the fact that the primary burden of change is on you and your clients. If this is an unreasonable expectation, it is probably wise to work toward a special placement for the child in a program that is staffed and organized to provide individualized help. Additionally, public and private schools have come to be slightly suspicious of efforts to claim students have a learning disability in order to gain special treatment, including the right to take untimed SAT exams (Rosenfeld and Wise 2000). Therapists can work best with the schools by demonstrating respect for the school's priorities and the willingness to be patient in developing a working relationship.

The youngster who is chemically dependent poses a special problem to the office therapist. The illness itself leads to denial, distortion, and outright lying. Since the primary source of information comes from the client, the therapist is often misled. Add to this the fact that chemical dependency detracts from the capacity to form the intimate and intense bond required for effective psychotherapy and the stage is set for a therapeutic failure.

School difficulties and substance abuse are often connected (Thompson et al. 1997) especially as substance abuse usually leads to truancy. A high index of suspicion is advised during the

The Office Therapist and School Problems

evaluation of any youngster referred for school difficulties. Some of the behaviors that should serve as red flags are discussed in Chapter 8. If the therapist can make the diagnosis, then appropriate treatment can be planned.

When the pattern of abuse or dependence is established, the question of family involvement comes up at once. Often, the parents have had suspicions, but frequently they do not and are themselves involved in denial of the problem. In the latter situation, the therapist is in a tough spot. One cannot collude with the youngster's self-destructive life style, but if the therapist abruptly tells the parents of the drug involvement, the young person may view this as a betrayal of trust. One should never extend the promise of total confidentiality to a minor since information about suicidal plans or homicidal intentions must be disclosed. Heavy drug use does not pose such an imminent danger, but in time can be equally disastrous. Since the basic underpinning of office psychotherapy is the development of an alliance, one can take some time in an effort to gain the young client's permission to enlist the parents in the battle to ameliorate the drug problem. It is a difficult job. Denial is a powerful opponent, especially when buttressed by the developmentally driven sense of personal omnipotence that accompanies adolescence. Sometimes the youngster will accept a challenge.

> *Harry was convinced that his heavy drug use had nothing to do with his academic collapse in his high school sophomore year. He stated that his poor school performance was related to his disgust with the driven American culture and his determination to forge a more "humane and natural" way of life. He stated that his drug use was entirely under his control and was part of his effort to gain enlightenment.*
>
> *The therapist challenged him to stop drugs completely for one month and keep a journal of his thoughts and reactions. Since Harry had considerable intellectual curiosity and a genuine desire to work in therapy, he took the dare.*

THE LEARNING ALLIANCE

After only two weeks he came to a session somewhat sheepish but ready to laugh at himself.

"Okay, I'm seeing things differently like you knew that I would. The real clincher was when one of my "druggy" buddies said, 'Damn, Harry. I never thought that a guy who was hooked like you could stop!' I guess everybody knew but me."

Harry's path to sobriety was not easy. He relapsed several times but never relinquished his resolve to give up drugs. Without any prompting he decided to tell his parents about his struggle and to ask for their help.

Membership in a twelve-step program may be helpful for many youngsters with drug problems. However, the therapist needs to be familiar with available meetings in the youngster's community. Some meetings do not welcome young people. Others are poorly run and may even attract drug dealers and other predators who increase the risk of dangerous behavior. Current and accurate information in this regard is usually available from drug counselors who work in programs for young people.

These individuals also may be helpful in recommending and assisting in the placement of youngsters who cannot bring their drug use into therapy and into the family. If there is no genuine progress, particularly if the drug use is still a family secret, the therapist has to face the need for unilateral action. If referral to an outpatient or residential drug treatment program is necessary, the parents obviously have to be involved. The young patient can be offered the chance to attend the meeting with the parents and even to present the need for more intensive therapy. However, the therapist must be present to ensure that the facts about the illness and the referral are presented accurately.

The therapist has to use clinical judgment in deciding whether to continue with office treatment or to insist on more intensive treatment. This judgment call is difficult in the case of adolescents who live in areas where drug use is endemic. All adolescents have some need to fit in with their peers and to appear somewhat rebellious to-

The Office Therapist and School Problems

ward adults. Occasional drug use is not indicative of abuse or dependence in adolescents. However, youngsters who are only using "socially" rarely show academic collapse, massive changes in friendship patterns, or truancy. They also tend to be pretty honest about their drug-using behavior in therapy.

The office therapy of school problems has its complications. However, if the therapist is willing to engage youngsters in an honest appraisal of their school attitudes and experiences, success is possible. The challenge is real since this is the setting where most problems are presented in their early stages, when they can most easily and quickly be resolved.

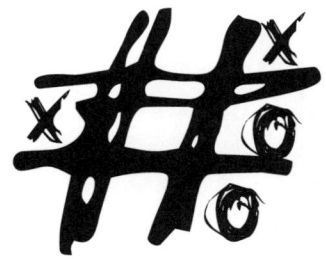

What do we do now?

12

Tying It All Together

We hope we have included all the essential people necessary to help students with emotional disturbance succeed in school. No matter what label we put on them — "disturbed," "troubled," "socially maladjusted," "behaviorally disordered," "delinquent," and "students in distress" — they need our help. We now leave the challenge to you. The fact that you've read this book means that you care about "our" students and you want to help. There is no one treatment, no one formula, no one recipe to help our youngsters succeed in school and life. Although we have provided strategies and case studies, adapt your approach to treat each troubled student as a unique individual with unique problems. The Victors, Tanyas, Charmains, Monroes, Roberts, Carlys, Arthurs, and the many others will appreciate the individual, customized attention and support.

As we review the AIM approach one last time, we are enclosing annotated homework assignments for key professionals and the team serving troubled students.

THE LEARNING ALLIANCE

ASPIRATION

Therapists
- Find and rework earlier school traumas
- Identify internal processes that have distracted the learning process
- Clearly define and enthusiastically present the advantages of learning
- Help the student identify their learning style in collaboration with teachers
- Model academic endeavor and be actively involved in the student's academic efforts

Teachers
- Identify and support the student's academic strengths
- Review the student's school history to understand past successes and failures
- Build on the student's interests
- Be enthusiastic and passionate about the learning and teaching process
- Provide individualized instruction to meet the student's social, emotional, and academic needs by using a variety of teaching methodologies, conducting ongoing formal and informal assessment, providing feedback and correction, reteaching when necessary and making sure there is sufficient reward and reinforcement.

Paraprofessionals
- Explore, observe, and identify the student's learning style and learning patterns
- Teach acceptable and appropriate school-ready behaviors and explain their purpose
- Support the value of education with the learning alliance team
- Model enthusiasm for learning
- Provide mentoring and support

Tying It All Together

Parents and Guardians
- Stress the importance of education for now and the future so your child views education in a positive light
- Help your child understand that success requires hard work but they can expect help from parents and school staff
- Help your child understand that school can sometimes be frustrating
- Support your child when s/he likes or hates school; help them understand that this is a natural response to school
- Believe that you are central to your child's education

Inspiration

Therapists
- Have the student list his/her strengths
- Teach self-efficacy skills
- Encourage independent thinking and behaviors
- Help the student discover s/he has the skills to succeed in school
- Affirm all achievements

Teachers
- In collaboration with the therapist, have the student identify his/her strengths using a strength-based approach to learning; students know what they don't do well, they need to know what they *can* do
- Teach appropriate and situational social-skills to students
- Encourage students to complete classwork independently
- Focus on the basic skills of reading, writing, and math

Paraprofessionals
- Help the student discover his/her strengths and weaknesses
- Compliment the student when s/he does something well or correctly

THE LEARNING ALLIANCE

- Support students in academic tasks as needed, but give students opportunities to attempt classwork independently
- Support the student's individualized educational program

Parents and Guardians
- Call attention to your child's strengths in the home, school, and community
- Frequently give your child praise and positive feedback
- Complete "spot checks" on your child's homework and verify with a telephone call to the teacher
- Relate to your child that you believe they have the skills to succeed in school

Mobilization

Therapists
- Have the student relate successful and unsuccessful strategies used for coping with academic and social challenges
- Help the student learn to compartmentalize conflict and personal concerns while remaining at least partly productive in the classroom
- Continue to be available to discuss ongoing failures as well as successes in school

Teachers
- Provide opportunities for the student to demonstrate his/her new found strengths and skills in the classroom when appropriate
- Telephone parents to relate positive school experiences
- Give student opportunities to self-correct their work so they learn to be constructive without being destructive

.Paraprofessionals
- Take the opportunity to tell a student you recognize their strengths

Tying It All Together

- Observe and identify the student's independent learning skills
- Maintain the student's newfound academic confidence by being available during crises, moments of self-doubt, and as appropriate to avoid establishing a codependent relationship in the learning alliance

Parents and Guardians
- Show an interest in your child's school/class projects
- Telephone the school to relate a positive event in the family, church, or community
- Work with the school in establishing appropriate educational and social goals and objectives for your child at regular meetings

Final Assignment
Our final assignment is to the team as a whole:
- Provide a model of cooperative efforts
- Share insights with the other team members and
- Provide support to other team members.

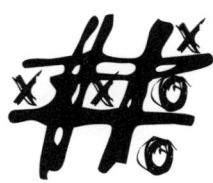

Bibliography

Abidin, R. R., and C. A. Kmetz. 1997. Teacher-student interactions as predicted by teaching stress and the perceived quality of the student-teacher relationship. Paper presented at the annual meeting of the National Association of School Psychologists, Anaheim, CA, April 3, 1997. ERIC No. ED 413 330.

Abikoff, H., and R. Gittelman. 1985. The normalizing effects of methylphenidate on classroom behavior of ADHD children. *Journal of Abnormal Child Psychology* 13: 33-44.

Allen, F.H. 1963. *Positive Aspects of Child Psychiatry.* New York: W.W. Norton.

Allen, J. D. 1986. Classroom management: Student's perspectives, goals, and strategies. *American Educational Research Journal* 23(3):437-459.

Anderson, E. 1999. *Code of the street.* New York: W.W. Norton.

———. 1997. Violence and the inner city street code. In Violence and childhood in the inner city, edited by Joan McCord. New York: Cambridge University Press.

Bagwell, C. L., B. S. G. Molina, W. E. Pelham, and B. Hoza. 2001. Attention-deficit hyperactivity disorder and problems in peer relations: Predictions from childhood to adolescence. *Journal of the American Academy of Child and Adolescent Psychiatry* 40(11):1285-1292.

Bandura, A. 1997. *Self-efficacy: The exercise of control.* New York. Freeman.

Barga, N. K.1996. Students with learning disabilities in education: Managing a disability. *Journal of Learning Disabilities* 29:413-421.

Barrett, M., and T. Trevitt. 1991. *Attachment behaviour and the school child: An introduction to education and therapy.* London: Routeledge

Berger M. and H. Kennedy. 1975. Pseudobackwardness in children: Maternal attitudes as an etiological factor. *Psychoanalytic Study of the Child* 30:279-306.

Beitchman, J. H., et al. 1998. Practice parameters for the assessment and treatment of children and adolescents with language and learning disorders. *Journal of the American Academy of Child and Adolescent Psychiatry* 30:10 Supplement 46S-62S.

Berkovitz, I. H. 1995. The adolescent in the schools: A therapeutic guide. *Adolescent Psychiatry* 20:343-363.

Berlinger, D. C., and B. J. Biddle. 1995. *The manufactured crisis: Myths, fraud and the attack on America's public schools.* Reading, MA: Addison-Wesley

Bibliography

Blanchard, P. 1946. Psychoanalytic contributions to the problems of reading disabilities. *Psychoanalytic Study of the Child* 2:163-187.

Bluestein, J. 1993. *Parents, teens and boundaries.* Deerfield Beach, FL: Health Commuinication, Inc.

Bodine, J. C., A. Olivarez,.and J. A. Ponticell. 2000. Adjudicated students' perceptions of ideal teacher characteristics. Paper presented at the annual meeting of the Southwest Educational Research Association, Dallas, TX, January 27-29, 2000. ERIC No. ED 440 320.

Brantlinger, E. 1994. High-income and low-income adolescents' view of special education. *Journal of Adolescent Research.* 9:384-407.

Bregman, R. 1999. Career and vocational education for special needs students. Presentation at Society for Applied Learning Technology Annual Conference, Arlington, VA, July 24-29.

Bregman, R. 1976. Vocational education: An alternative rehabilitation mode for correctional institutions. In *Vocational Education for Special Groups,* edited by James E. Wall. Washington, DC: American Vocational Education.

Budney, A. J., J. R. Hughes, B. A. Moore, and P. L. Navy. 2001. Marijuana abstinence effects in marijuana smokers maintained in their home environment. *Archives of General Psychiatry* 58:917-924.

Chambers, J.C. 1999. Youth caught in the enchanting web of chemicals. *Reclaiming Children and Youth* 8:34-38.

Chess, S, .and A. Thomas. 1986. *Temperament in clinical practice.* New York: Guilford Press.

Clark, H. B., M. E. Prange, B. Lee, A. Boyd, B. A. McDonald, and E.

S. Stewart. 1994. Improving adjustment outcomes for foster children with emotional and behavioral disorders: Early findings from a controlled study of individualized services. *Journal of Emotional and Behavioral Disorders* 2:207-218.

Cohen, J. 1985. Learning disabilities and adolescence: Developmental considerations. *Adolescent Psychiatry* 12:177-195.

——————. 1993. Attentional disorders in adolescence: Integrating psychoanalytic and neuropsychological diagnostic and developmental considerations. *Adolescent Psychiatry* 19:301-342.

——————. 1997. On the uses and misuses of psychoeducational evaluations. *Adolescent Psychiatry* 21:253-268.

Denney, C., and M. D. Rapport. 1993. Predicting methylphenidate response in children with ADHD: Theoretical, empirical, and conceptual models. *Journal of the American Academy of Child and Adolescent Psychiatry* 38:393-401.

Director, L. 2000. Understanding and treating adolescent substance use: Systems, families, and individual meaning. *Journal of Infant, Child, and Adolescent Psychotherapy* 1:97-110.

DuPaul, G. J., and M. D. Rapport. 1993. Does methylphenidate normalize the classroom performance of children with attention deficit disorder? *Journal of the American Academy of Child and Adolescent Psychiatry* 32 (SS).

Eggert, L. L., J. R. Herting, E. A. Thompson, L. J. Nicholas, and B. Dicker. 1992. Preventing adolescent drug involvement, school dropout and emotional distress. Paper presented at the annual American Public Health Association convention, November, 1992.

Bibliography

Eggert, L. 1994. *Anger management for youth: Stemming aggression and violence.* Bloomington, IN: National Educational Service

Fingarette, H. 1988. *Heavy drinking.* Berkeley: University of California Press.

Forness, S. R., and J. Knitzer. 1992. A new proposed definition and terminology to replace "serious emotional disturbance" in Individuals with Disabilities Education Act. *School Psychology Review* 21:12-30.

Freud, A. 1965. *Normality and pathology in childhood: Assessments of development.* New York: International Universities Press.

Fried, S., and F. P. Fried. 1996. *Bullies and victims.* New York: Evans & Company.

Furlong, M., G. Morrison, and J. Dear. 1994 Addressing School Violence as Part of School's Educational Mission. *Preventing School Failure.* 38:10-17.

Garber, B. 1992. The learning disabled adolescent: A clinical perspective. *Adolescent Psychiatry* 18:322-347.

Geschwind, N. 1983. Biological associations of left-handedness. *Annals of Dyslexia* 33: 29-40.

Golding, W. 1959. *Lord of the flies.* Berkely: Berkely Publishing Group.

Goldstein, A. P. 1987. *Aggression replacement training: A comprehensive intervention for aggressive youth.* Champaign, IL: Research Press.

Greene, R. 2001. *The explosive child.* New York: Quill

Habel, J., L. A. Bloom, M. S. Ray, and E. Bacon. 1999. Consumer reports: What students with behavior disorders say about school. *Remedial and Special Education* 20(2), 93-105.

Hare, R. D. 1998. Psychopathy, affect and behavior. In *Psychopathy: Theory, research and implications for society*, edited by D. J. Cooke, A. E. Forth, and R. D. Hare. Dordrecht: The Netherlands: Kluwer Academic. NATO Asi series; Series D, Behavioral and Social Sciences No. 88:105-137

Harrell, A. 1996. Intervening with high-risk youth. Preliminary findings from the children-at-risk program. National Institute of Justice Research Preview. Department of Justice, Washington, DC.

Hazler, R. J. 1996. *Breaking the cycle of violence: Interventions for bullying and victimization*. Washington, DC: Accelerated Development.

Jellinek, E. M. 1960. *The disease concept of alcoholism*. New Haven: Hillhouse Press.

Kaler, S., A. Sacclaris, and C. Weddington-Ruhl. 2000. *Standards and Expectations for The Foundation School Staff*. Rockville, MD: The Foundation Schools.

Kauffman, J. M. 2001. *Characteristics of emotional and behavioral disorders of children and youth*. Columbus, OH: Merril Prentice Hall.

Kennedy, R. L., and J. H. Morton. 1999. *A school for healing: Alternative strategies for teaching at-risk students*. New York: Peter Lange Publishing.

Kraiser, S. 1996. *The safe child book: A common approach to protecting children and teaching children to protect themselves*. New York: Simon and Schuster.

Bibliography

Kress, J. S. and M. J. Elias. 1993. Substance abuse prevention in special education populations: Review and recommendations. *Journal of Special Education* 27: 35-52.

Kunert, K. and T. Marnell. 2002. *Another Path: Substance Abuse Chart.* Rockville, MD: The Foundation Schools.

Lalemand, K. 2002. *Non-abusive psychological and physical intervention (NAPPI) International.* Great Barrington, MA: Eagleton School.

Langer, E., A. Piper, and J. Friedus. 1986. *Preventing mindlessness: A positive side of dyslexia.* Cambridge: Harvard University.

Lear, J. G., B. H. Gleicher, A. St.Germaine, and R. J. Porter. 1991. Reorganizing health care for adolescents: The experience of the school-based adolescent health care program. *Journal of Adolescent Health* 12:450-458.

Leone, P. E., P. G. Luttig, S. Zlotlow, and E. J. Trickett. 1990. Understanding the social ecology of classrooms for adolescents with behavioral disorders: A preliminary study of differences in perceived environments. *Behavioral Disorders* 16(1):55-65.

Lombardi, D. 2000. *The Foundation Schools Four Cornerstones.* Rockville, MD: The Foundation Schools.

Long, N., M. M. Wood, and F. A. Fecser. 2001. *Life space crisis intervention: Talking with students in conflict.* Austin, TX: PRO-ED, Inc.

Lovitt, T. C., M. Plavins and S. Cushing. 1999. What do pupils with disabilities have to say about their experience in high school. *Remedial and Special Education* 20(2):67-83.

Lunenberg, F. C., and L. J. Schmidt. 1989. Pupil control ideology, pupil control behavior, and the quality of school life. *Journal of Research and Development in Education.* 22(4): 36-44.

Mahler, M. S., F. Pine, and A. Berghan. 1975. *The psychoanalytic birth of the human infant: Symbiosis and individuation.* New York: Basic Books.

Markowitz, I. 1975. Making meaningful advice to parents acceptable. *International Journal of Group Psychotherapy* 25: 323-329.

Meeks, J.E., and W. Bernet. 2001. *The fragile alliance.* Malabar, FL: Kreiger Publishing.

Meloy, J. R., A. G. Hempel, K. Mohandie, A. A. Shiva, and B. T. Gray. 2001. Offender and offense characteristics of a nonrandom sample of adolescent mass murders. *Journal of the American Academy of Child and Adolescent Psychiatry* 44(6): 719-731.

Millington, T. and B. Molloy. 1998. The teacher and the therapist within: A dialogue. *International Annals of Adolescent Psychiatry* 1:140-151.

Minuchin, S., B. Montalvo, B. G. Guerney, B. L. Rosman, and F. Schumer. 1967. *Families of the slums.* New York: Basic Books

Moeller, F. G., E. S. Barratt, D. M. Dougherty, J. M Schmitz, and A. C. Swann. 2001. Psychiatric aspects of impulsivity. *American Journal of Psychiatry* 158(11): 1783-1793.

Moore, K. J., and P. Chamberlain. 1994. Treatment foster care: Toward development of community-based models for adolescents with severe emotional and behavioral disorders. *Journal of Emotional and Behavioral Disorders* 2:22-30.

Newman, D., A. Horne, and C. Bartolomucci. 2000. *Bully Busters: A*

Bibliography

teacher's manual for helping bullies, victims and bystanders. Champaign, IL: Research Press NIDA. 1999. Monitoring the Future Survey. National Institute on Drug Abuse, Washington, DC.

Olweus, D. 1994. Annotation — Bullying at school: Basic facts and effects of a school based intervention program. *Journal of Child Psychology and Psychiatry* 35:1171-1190.

Parens, H. 1975. Parenthood as a developmental phase. *Journal of the American Psychoanalytic Association* 23:154-165.

Parese, S. 1997. *Therapeutic aggression control techniques (TACT-2)*. 2d ed. Washington, DC: S. Pares.

Peck, M. S. 1983. *People of the lie*. New York: Simon and Schuster.

Podorefsky, D. L., M. McDonald-Dowdell, and W. R. Beardslee. 2001. Adaptation of preventive interventions for a low-income, culturally diverse community. *Journal of the American Academy of Child and Adolescent Psychiatry* 40(8):879-886.

Pope, H. G., A. J. Gruber, J. I. Hudson, M. A. Huestis, and D. Yurgelun-Todd. 2001. Neuropsychological performance in long-term cannabis users. *Archives of General Psychiatry* 58:909-915.

Porac, C., and S. Coren. 1981. *Lateral preferences and human behavior*. New York: Springer.

Rappaport, N. 2001. Psychiatric consultation to school-based health centers: Lessons learned in an emerging field. *Journal of the American Academy of Child and Adolescent Psychiatry* 40(12):1473-1475.

Reneman, L., J. Lavalaye, B. Schmand, F. A. de Wolff, W. van den Brink, G. J. den Heeten, and J. Booij. 2001. Cortical serotonin transporter density and verbal memory in individuals who stopped using 3, 4-methylenedioxymethamphetamine (MDMA or "Ecstasy"). *Archives of General Psychiatry* 58:901-908.

Robinson, L. H. 1990. In defense of parents. *Adolescent Psychiatry* 17:36-50.

Rogers, C. R. 1969. *Freedom to learn.* Columbus, OH: Charles E. Merrill.

Ronan, K. R. and P. C. Kendall. 1990. Non-self-controlled adolescents: Applications of cognitive-behavioral therapy. *Adolescent Psychiatry* 17:479-505.

Ross, D. M. 1996. *Childhood bullying and teasing: What school personnel and other professionals, and parents can do.* Alexandria, VA: American Counseling Association.

Rosenfeld, A., and N. Wise. 2000. *Hyper-parenting: Are you hurting your child by trying too hard?* New York: St. Martin's Press.

Silver, A. A., and R. A. Hagin. 1985. Outcomes of Learning Disabilities in Adolescence. *Adolescent Psychiatry* 12:197-213.

Smucker, K. S., J. M. Kauffman, and D. W. Ball. 1996. School-related problems of special education loster care students with emotional or behavioral disorders: Comparison to other groups. *Journal of Emotional and Behavioral Disorders* 4:30-39.

Snyder, C. R. 1994. *The psychology of hope: You can get there from here.* New York: Free Press.

Stanton, M. and T. Todd. 1982. *The family of drug abuse and addiction.* New York: Guilford.

Strayhorn, J. M. 2002. Self-control: Toward systematic training pro-

Bibliography

grams. *Journal of the American Academy of Child and Adolescent Psychiatry* 41(1):17-27.

Strayhorn, J. M. 2002. Self-control: Theory and research. *Journal of the American Academy of Child and Adolescent Psychiatry* 41(1):7-16.

Sugar, M. 1993. Education and poverty: Problems and possibilities. *Adolescent Psychiatry* 19:31-45.

Sykes, C. J. 1995. *Dumbing down our kids: Why American children feel good about themselves but can't read, write or add.* New York: St. Martin's Griffin.

Thompson, E. A., M. Horn, J. R. Hertling, and L. L. Eggert. 1997. Enhancing outcomes in an indicated drug prevention program for high-risk youth. *Journal of Drug Education* 27:19-41.

Twemlow, S. W., P. Fonagy, and F. C. Sacco. 2001. A social systems-power dynamics approach to preventing school violence. In *School violence: Assessment, management, prevention* edited by M. Shafii, and S. L. Shafii. Washington, DC: American Psychiatric Publishing.

U. S. Department of Labor. 2000. *National compensation survey: Occupational wages in the U. S. 2000.* Washington, DC: Bureau of Labor Statistics.

U. S. Postal Service. 2002. *USPS Human Resources Website:* www.ups.com/hrisp

Weissman, S., and R. S. Cohen, R.S. 1985. The parenting alliance and adolescence. *Adolescent Psychiatry* 12:24-45.

Whitfield, J. 1993. *Boundaries and relationships: Knowing, protecting*

THE LEARNING ALLIANCE

and enjoying the self. Deerfield Beach, FL: Health Communications, Inc.

Wood, M. M. and N. J. Long. 1991. *Life space intervention.* Austin, TX: Pro-Ed, Inc.

Resources

Resources for Teachers

The Acting Out Child: Coping with Classroom Disruption
Hill M. Walker (1995)

Antisocial Behavior in School: Strategies and Best Practices
Hill Walker, G. Colvin, and E. Ramsey (1990)

Behavioral Disorders (Journal published by CCBD)
Beyond Behavior (Published by CCBD)
Council for Children with Behavior Disorders
The Council of Exceptional Children

Building Classroom Discipline
C. M. Charles (1996)

THE LEARNING ALLIANCE

Characteristics of Emotional & Behavioral Disorders of Children and Youth
James M. Kauffman (2001)

Children Who Hate
Fritz Redl (1951) (a classic, out of print, but some copies are available through Amazon.com)

Comprehensive Classroom Management: Creating Positive Learning Environments for All Students
by V. F. Jones and L. S. Jones (1995)

Conferencing with Parents of Exceptional Children
R. Simpson (1990)

Conflict in the Classroom: The Education of At-risk and Troubled Students
Nicholas Long and William Morse (1996)

Delinquents on Delinquency
Arnold Goldstein (1990)

Educating Students with Behavior Disorders
M. S. Rosenberg (1997)

Emotional and Behavioral Disorders: A 25 Year Focus
R. J. Whelan (1998)

Emotional Intelligence
Daniel Goleman (1995)

150 Ways to Increase Intrinsic Motivation in the Classroom
J. P. Raffini (1996)

Making Placement Decisions: Constructing Appropriately Restrictive Environments for Students with Emotional and Behavioral Disorders
Steve R. Braaten and James M. Kauffman (2000)

Resources

Reclaiming Children and Youth: The Journal of Strength-based Interventions
Nicholas J. Long and Larry K. Brendtro, Editors (NEED YEAR)

Reclaiming Youth at Risk: Our Hope for the Future
Larry K. Brendtro, Martin Brokenleg, and Steve Van Bockern (1990)

A School for Healing: Alternative Strategies for Teaching At-Risk Students
R. L. Kennedy and J. H. Morgan (1999)

Understanding Troubled and Troubling Youth
Peter Leone (1990)

Waging Peace in Our Schools
Linda Lantieri and Janet Patti (1996)

Resources for Parents and Guardians

Best Friends, Worse Enemies: Understanding the Social Lives of Children
Michael Thompson, Catherine O'Neil Grace, and Lawrence Cohen (2001)

Creating Emotionally Safe Schools
Jane Bluestein (2001)

Emotionally Intelligent Parenting: How to Raise a Self-Disciplined, Responsible, Socially Skilled Child
By Maurice J. Elias, Stephen E. Tobias, and Brian S. Friedlander (1999)

The Explosive Child
Ross Greene (2001)

Golden Rules for Parenting: A Child Psychiatrist Discovers the Bible
Dan Myers (1998)

THE LEARNING ALLIANCE

Honorable Intentions: A Parent's Guide to Educational Planning for Children with Emotional or Behavioral Disorders.
D. Jordan (1995)

The Hurried Child: Growing up Too Fast Too Soon
David Elkind (1988)

I Know My Child Can Do Better
Anne Rambo (2002)

A Mind at a Time
Mel Levine, MD (2002)

Overcoming Underachieving
Ruth Peters (2000)

Parents Under Siege: Why You are the Solution and not the Problem in Your Child's Life
James Garbarino (2001)

The Romance of Risk: Why Teenagers Do the Things They Do
Lynn Ponton (1997)

Schools That Learn
Peter Senge (2000)

Teens in Turmoil: A Path to Change for Parents, Adolescents and their Families
Carol Maxym and Leslie B. York (2000)

Resources for Dealing with Bullies

Aggression Replacement Training: A Comprehensive Intervention for Aggressive Youth (Rev. Ed.).
A. P. Goldstein, B. Glick, and J. C. Gibbs (1998)

Resources

Annotation — Bullying at school: Basic facts and effects of a school based intervention program. *Journal of Child Psychology and Psychiatry* 35: 1171-1190
D. Olweus (1994)

Breaking the Cycle of Violence: Interventions for Bullying and Victimization
R. J. Hazler (1996)

Bullies and Victims
S. Fried and P. F. Fried (1996)

Bully Busters: A Teacher's Manual for Helping Bullies, Victims and Bystanders
D. Newman, A. Horne, and C. Bartolomucci, (2000)

Childhood Bullying and Teasing: What School Personnel, other Professionals and Parents Can Do
D. M. Ross (1996)

The Prepare Curriculum: Teaching Prosocial Competencies (Rev. Ed.)
A. P. Goldstein (1999)

The Safe Child Book: A Common Approach to Protecting Children and Teaching Children to Protect Themselves
S. Kraiser (1996)

Index

A
Abusive relationships, 111
Academic failure, behaviors predictive of, 40
Academic success
    behaviors predictive of, 40
    drug use and, 96
    family and, 67–78
    learning disabilities as barriers to, 36–37
    psychological requirements for, 1–2
    review of, with student, 59–61
    rewards of, obstacles to, 22–23
    and work experience, 18–19
Adolescents
    behavior of, in peer groups vs. adult company, 127–128
    with clear boundaries, 53
    decision-making and, 116–117
    drug use and, 95, 104

goal-setting by, 63
identity formation in, 9
independence of, 127
learning disabilities among, 36–37
parents of, 69
rebellion during, 60–61
self-esteem in, 9
waypower of, 65
willpower of, 64
Adoptive parents, 76–78
Adults. *See also* Parent(s); Teacher(s)
influences on students, 4, 9
Aggression Replacement Therapy (ART), 128
Aggressive bullying, 118
AIM, xxiii
Anger, as disguise for embarrassment, 45
Anger Management for Youth, 128
Another Path (drug treatment program), 105
Anxiety, as distraction from learning, 3
Apprenticeships, 19
ART. See Aggression Replacement Therapy
Aspiration, 4–5
definition of, xxiii, 4
example of, 20–21
office therapists and, 140–141
paraprofessionals and, 152
parents/guardians and, 153
peers and, 7
teachers and, 152
therapists and, 152
Athletics, academic success and, 19
Attachment Behavior and the Schoolchild (Barrett and Trevitt), 6–7
Attachment theory, 6–7
Attendance, drug use and, 94
Attention disorders

Index

as distraction from learning, 3
secondary deficits with, 4
treatment of, 3–4

B

Bad days, permission to have, 58
Behavior disorders
    definition of, 12
    drug use and, 93–105
    strategies for dealing with, 51
Beliefs, as cornerstone of learning community, 122
Big Brothers, parenting roles in, 77
Blaming
    of parents, 67–68
    of victims, in bullying, 111
Boundary(ies)
    clear
        characteristics of students with, 53
        obstacles to, 54
    definition of, 52
    paraprofessionals and, 131–133
    romantic relationships and, 131–132
    in student-teacher relationships, 48–50
Bravery, 108
Bullying, 109–112
    aggressive, 118
    direct work with, 112
    interventions for, 119–120
    limiting of, 8
    motivation in, 110
    participants in, 109–110
    passive, 118
    power dynamics in, 109
    prevention of, 119–120
    resources for dealing with, 172–173

social, 109
victims of, 110–111
Bus drivers/bus aides, 136
Bystanders, of bullying, 109–110

C
Career development, 23
Chemical dependency. *See* Drug use
Children of the chemically dependent (COCD), 96
Church programs, parenting roles in, 77
Class changes, due to teacher conflicts, 44–45
COCD. *See* Children of the chemically dependent
Code of the Street (Anderson), 107, 127–128
Commitment, maintenance of, 57–65
Community meetings, 115
Community outreach programs, parenting roles in, 77
Confidence, xxiii–xxiv. *See also* Inspiration
    in ability to learn, 32–36
    in achievement of future plans, 21
Confidentiality, 147
Consistency, as cornerstone of learning community, 122–123
Contests, in drug prevention programs, 96
Countertransference, in drug treatment programs, 101
Crisis
    aftermath of, 113–114
    responses to, 112–113
Crushes. *See* Boundary(ies)

D
Decision-making, student involvement in, 116–117
Denial, drug use and, 100, 147
Dependency
    rejection of, 5
    in student-teacher relationships, 49–50
Depression, as distraction from learning, 3

Index

Discipline management, 44
Drug-free school environment, creation of, 94–98
Drug prevention programs
    fear tactics in, 95
    school-based, 93–94
    staff involvement in, 96–97
    strategies in, 96
Drug treatment programs, 100–101, 148–149
    example of, 105
    family involvement in, 103
    group therapy in, 100–101
    inpatient, 101–102
    school-based, 93–94
Drug use, 93–105
    and academic achievement, 96
    among adolescents, 95, 104
    and attendance, 94
    cultural acceptance of, 97
    denial of, 100, 147
    in elementary school, 95
    family and, 147
    in high school, 95
    identification of students with, 98
    impact of, 99–102
    in middle school, 95
    office therapist and, 146–149
    by parents, 96
    peer groups and, 99
    pseudo-individuation and, 94
    relapse of, 102
    by staff, 97
    by therapists, 101
Dumbing Down Our Kids (Sykes), 44
Dyslexia, as distraction from learning, 3

E

Education. *See* School
Education level, and salaries, 18, 25–27
Elementary school
    drug issues in, 95
    reinforcements in, 116
Embarrassment, anger as disguise for, 45
Emotional competence, development of, 5–6
Emotional disorders
    and academic self-esteem, 59
    definition of, 12
    strategies for dealing with, 51
Emotional disturbance, IDEA definition of, 11
Emotionally immature students, and student-teacher conflicts, 47–48
Entertainment arts, academic success and, 19
Ethics, 108
Expectations
    realism of, 2
    setting of, 57–58
    for students, 58
    for teachers, 89–90
    for therapists, 87–88
The Explosive Child (Greene), 3

F

False accusations, of inappropriate sexual behavior, 132
Family, 67–78. *See also* Parent(s)
    drug use and, 103, 147
Family conflict, dislike of school as expression of, 35–36
Family therapy, 74
Feedback, positive, 75
Fighting, 112–113
Foster parents, 76–78
The Foundation School, xxii

Index

Freedom to Learn (Rogers), 82
Future plans, of students, 21–22

G
Geographic moves, drug use and, 99
Goals
    development of, 63
    hope and, 62
    setting of, 57–58
Group homes, 77
Group meetings, 115
Group therapy, in drug treatment programs, 100–101
Guardians. *See also* Parent(s)
    and aspiration, 153
    and inspiration, 154
    knowledge of school experiences of, 30
    and mobilization, 155
    and progress reviews, 59–60
    strategies for, 74–76

H
High school, drug use in, 95
Higher education, alternatives to, 19
Home environment, 60
Homework. See Schoolwork
Honor students, drug use and, 96
Hope
    definition of, 62
    nurturing, 63
    restoration of, 57–65
Humanistic approach, to discipline management, 44

I
Identity formation, in adolescents, 9
IEP. *See* Individualized Education Plan

IEP Team, 73
Independence, of adolescents, 127
Individuality, 2–3
Individualized Education Plan (IEP), 73–74
Individuals with Disabilities Education Act (IDEA), emotional disturbance definition in, 11
Infatuations. *See* Boundary(ies)
Inpatient drug treatment programs, 101–102
Inspiration, 5, xxiv
    definition of, 4, xxiii
    office therapists and, 141–142
    paraprofessionals and, 153–154
    parents/guardians and, 154
    teachers and, 153
    therapists and, 153
Interventions, as cornerstone of learning community, 121–122

J
Janitors, 136
Job placements, from vocational programs, 23

K
Key events, 141

L
Labeling of students, dangers of, 7, 8–9
Language barriers, between therapists and paraprofessionals, 128
Learning
    as boring, 20
    personal value of *(See Aspiration)*
Learning alliance, structure of, xxi–xxii
Learning community
    characteristics of, 107–108
    cornerstones of, 121–123
    creation of, 108–112

Index

    maintenance of, 112–117
    play and socialization in, 115–116
Learning disabilities, as barriers to academic success, 36–37
Learning inhibitions, 2
Leisure activities, drug use and, 99–100
Life Space Crisis Intervention (LSCI), 128
Lord of the Flies (Golding), 107
LSCI. *See* Life Space Crisis Intervention

M

Maintenance personnel, 136
Manipulation, by students, 71–72
The Manufactured Crisis (Berliner and Biddle), 44
Mental attitudes, 4–9
Mental willpower, 62
Mentoring programs, parenting roles in, 77
Middle school, drug use in, 95
Minorities, apprenticeship opportunities for, 19
Mobilization, 5
    definition of, 4, xxiii
    paraprofessionals and, 154–155
    parents/guardians and, 155
    teachers and, 154
    therapists and, 154
Moral standards, in learning setting, 8
Morality, 108

N

NAPPI. *See* Non-Abusive Psychological and Physical Intervention
Negative attitudes
    towards school, 29–41
        evaluation of, 30–36
        identification of, 30–36
        reasons for, 38
        strategies to improve, 41

in students with disabilities, 39
towards teachers, 43–54
Negative leaders, among students, 114–115
Neurological disorders, as distraction from learning, 3
Non-Abusive Psychological and Physical Intervention (NAPPI), 129
Nonbiological parenting, 76–78

O

Occupational training, alternatives to, 19
Office therapists, 139–149, xxii
    and aspiration, 140–141
    drug treatment programs and, 146–149
    initial meetings with, 139–140
    and inspiration, 141–142
    relationship with parents, 139, 142–143
    relationship with school, 144–145
    therapeutic alliance with, 139
Outside agencies, 136

P

Paraprofessional(s), 125–136
    and aspiration, 152
    boundary issues and, 131–133
    and inspiration, 153–154
    knowledge of students, 126–128
    language barriers and, 128
    and mobilization, 154–155
    parenting roles of, 130–131
    respect for, 126–127
    therapeutic holds and, 128–130
    value of, 132–133
Parent(s), xxii–xxiii. *See also* Guardians
    acceptance of student problems by, 68
    and aspiration, 153
    awareness of school policies and procedures of, 72–73

Index

blaming of, 67–68
criticism of, by children, 75–76
drug use by, 96
influence over children, underestimation of, 143
and inspiration, 154
knowledge of school experiences of, 30
manipulation by children, 71
and mobilization, 155
nonbiological, 76–78
paraprofessionals as, 130–131
and progress reviews, 59–60
strategies for, 74–76
therapist as, 77–78
unavailable, 75
unfit, 75–76
Parent-school relationship, 68
  development of, 69–72
  foundation of, 69–70
  office therapists and, 144–145
Parent-therapist relationship
  office therapists and, 139, 142–143
  strategies offered in, 74–76
Parental surrogates, 75. *See also* Guardians
Passive bullying, 118
Peers
  acceptance by, 1–3
  acceptance of school by, 31–32
  aspiration and, 7
  drug use and, 99
People of the Lie (Peck), 67
Persistence, of therapist, 34
Personality conflicts, between teacher and student, 45–47
Physical restraints. See Therapeutic holds
Play, in learning community, 115–116
Positive attitude, importance of, 8

Positive feedback, 75
Power dynamics, in bullying, 109
Praise, 59
Program assistants. *See* Paraprofessional(s)
Pseudo-individuation, and drug use, 94
Psychotherapy
    academic issues in, 1–14
        history of, 13–14
        lack of emphasis on, xxi
        reasons for, 9–10
    objectives of, 1
Psychotic child, distraction from learning of, 3
Public Law 101-476. See Individuals with Disabilities Education Act
Punishment, suspension as, 68

R

Racism, and lack of academic success, 22–23
Rebellion, dislike of school as expression of, 35–36
Reinforcements, 115–117
Residential drug treatment programs, 101–102
Resources
    for dealing with bullies, 172–173
    for teachers, 169–172
Respect
    among students, 109
    as cornerstone of learning community, 121
    for paraprofessionals, 126–127
Rewards, types of, 116
Role models, lack of, 22–23
Romantic relationships, boundary issues and, 131–132

S

Safety, of school environment, 8
Salaries, education level and, 18, 25–27
School

Index

    commitment to individual children of, 70
    first experience of, 30
    negative attitudes towards, 29–41
        reasons for, 38
        strategies to improve, 41
        in students with disabilities, 39
    policies and procedures of, parental awareness of, 72–73
    psychotherapy in
        history of, 13–14
        lack of emphasis on, xxi
        reasons for, 9–10
    value of, 17–27
        student acknowledgment of, 108
School administrative assistant, 133
School environment
    drug-free, 94–98, 96–98
    safety of, 8
    student role in, 7–9
School failure. *See* Academic failure
School-parent relationship. *See* Parent-school relationship
School secretary, 133
School success. See Academic success
School-therapist relationship, 144–145
Schoolwork, in therapy sessions, 21, 33, 59, 141
Self-confidence, and vocational training, 23
Self-control, xxiii
Self-efficacy, xxiii–xxiv
Self-esteem
    in adolescents, 9
    emotional disorders and, 59
Sexual relationships, boundary issues and, 131–132
Skilled trades, 19
SLP. *See* Speech and language pathologist
Social acceptance, psychological requirements for, 1–2
Social bullying, 109

Social histories, in Individualized Education Plans, 73–74
Socialization, in learning community, 115–116
Socioeconomic status, and lack of academic success, 22–23
Speech and language pathologist (SLP), 133–136
Staff. *See also* Paraprofessional(s); Teacher(s)
    drug use and, 96–97, 97
Standards
    for teachers, 89–90
    for therapists, 87–88
Student(s)
    ability to learn of, confidence in, 32–36
    adult influences on, 4, 9
    boundaries and, 53
    criticism of parents by, 75–76
    decision-making and, 116–117
    expectations of, 58
    future plans of, 21–22
    goal-setting by, 58
    individual commitment to, 70
    manipulation by, 71–72
    need to prove themselves, 71
    negative leaders among, 114–115
    past history of, 70
    perceptions of teachers, 31
    respect among, 109
    review of progress with, 59–61
Student-teacher conflicts
    emotionally immature students and, 47–48
    personality conflicts and, 45–47
Student-teacher relationships
    boundary issues in, 48–50
    dependency in, 49–50
Students with disabilities, negative attitudes towards school among, 39
Substance abuse. *See* Drug use

Index

Support staff. *See* Paraprofessional(s)
Suspension, as punishment, 68
Symbols of mutual achievement, as rewards, 116

T

TACT-2. See Therapeutic Aggression Control Techniques
Teacher(s)
    and aspiration, 152
    collaboration with therapists, 81–90
        ideas for, 86
        roles in, 83–85
    conflicts with
        student role in, 45–48
        therapist role in, 43–44
    differences from therapists, 81–83
    and discipline management, 44
    and drug prevention programs, 96–97
    drug use by, 97
    expectations for, 89–90
    frustration of, 46
    and inspiration, 153
    and mobilization, 154
    negative attitudes towards, 43–54
    resources for, 169–172
    standards for, 89–90
    student perceptions of, 31
Teacher-student relationships. See Student-teacher relationships
Teamwork, with Individualized Education Plans, 73
Therapeutic Aggression Control Techniques (TACT-2), 129
Therapeutic alliance, with office therapists, 139
Therapeutic holds, 128–130
Therapeutic persistence, 34
Therapist(s). *See also* Office therapists
    and aspiration, 152
    collaboration with teachers, 81–90

        ideas for, 86
        roles in, 83–85
    differences from teachers, 81–83
    expectations for, 87–88
    and inspiration, 153
    and mobilization, 154
    parenting roles of, 77–78
    as recovering addicts, 101
    role in learning alliance, xxi–xxii
    role in student-teacher conflicts, 43–44
    schoolwork and, 21
    standards for, 87–88
Therapist-parent relationship, 74–76
Therapist-school relationship, 144–145
Therapy sessions
    schoolwork in, 33, 59, 141
    student history in, 70
Transference wish, 77
Twelve-step programs, 148

U
Unfit parents, 75–76

V
Victims, of bullying, 109–111, 119–120
Violence, 112–113
Visual overlay, 141
Vocational training, 19, 23
Volunteers, 136

W
Wages
    education level and, 18, 25–27
    as rewards, 116
    Waypower, 62, 65

Index

Willpower, 62, 63
Work experience, academic success and, 18–19

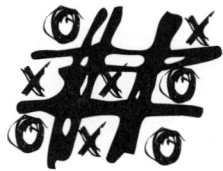

About the Authors

John E. Meeks, MD
Dr. Meeks has been a practicing child and adolescent psychiatrist for over forty-five years. He received his medical degree from the University of Tennessee. He has taught at the University of Texas Southwestern Medical School and the Georgetown University Medical School. He has served as director of several child and adolescent divisions in psychiatric hospitals. He is co-founder, and has served as the president and Medical Director of The Foundation Schools since 1975. The Foundation Schools operate four schools for students with emotional disturbance K-12. He has authored several articles on individual and group psychotherapy, behavior disorders of childhood, treatment of adolescent suicide, adolescent substance abuse, hospitalization and inpatient treatment and adolescent depression. Dr. Meeks is best known for his classic textbook *The Fragile Alliance* and another book on depression: *High Times, Low Times: The Many Faces of Adolescent Depression*. Dr. Meeks has presented nationally and internationally. In 1998 Dr. Meeks received the prestigious national Schonfeld Award

from the American Society for Adolescent Psychiatry for his lifetime contributions to child and adolescent psychiatry.

Philippe J. Dupont, EdD

Dr. Dupont has been working with children and adolescents for twenty-nine years. He has served as Associate Professor at The George Washington University teaching courses in assessment, behavior management, mainstreaming, diversity and behavior disorders. He has taught in private and public schools. He has taught for the Prince George's County Public Schools in Maryland, received his doctorate in Special Education from the George Washington University in 1985. He served as Principal and Education Director of The Pathways Schools for eleven years and Director of The Foundation School of Prince George's County for four years. He is also a consultant on staff development for orphanages in Bosnia and Herzegovina with Training Workshops International (TWI) for the Children. He presents workshops on various topics in special education at the state, national and international levels. He recently presented his work with the Bosnian orphanages at the United States Institute of Peace Conference at the Airlie Center in Warrenton, Virginia. He received the Rita Ives Outstanding Alumni Award from The George Washington University in 1995 for his contributions to the field of emotional disturbance. Dr. Dupont was president of the Maryland Association of Nonpublic Special Education Facilities (MANSEF) from 1997 — 1999. He has written articles about adolescents with emotional and behavioral problems. He is presently the Director of Public Relations for The Foundation Schools.

Spread the word and help students learn.

You can purchase additional copies of *The Learning Alliance* for friends and colleagues using the order form below, finding the book on Amazon.com or by calling 301-984-DMSP (301-984-3677).

[ ] **Yes**, I want ____ copies of *The Learning Alliance* for $19.95 ($27.00 Canadian) each plus applicable tax. ($14.95 each for orders of five or more). All proceeds will go to The Foundation Schools. Include $3.95 shipping and handling for one book and $1.95 for each additional book. Payment must accompany orders.

[ ] I would like to consider having Drs. Meeks and Dupont give a presentation or seminar for my school or organization. Please send me information.

[ ] My check or money order for $ ____ is enclosed.
[ ] Please charge my   [ ] Visa [ ] MasterCard

Name _____
Organization _____
Address _____
City _____ State _____ Zip _____
Phone _____ Email _____
Card # _____ Expiration ___ / ___ / ___
Signature _____

Make your check payable to:

DMS Press
6000 Executive Blvd. #605
Rockville, MD 20852
www.learningalliance.org
Fax: 301-881-5118